Napoleon & St Helena

Napoleon & St Helena

On the Island of Exile

by
Johannes Willms

Translated by John Brownjohn

Armchair Traveller
at the bookHaus

First published in German by marebuchverlag, Hamburg/Germany in 2007 under the title
St Helena.

Copyright © 2007 by Johannes Willms

© 2007 by marebuchverlag, Hamburg/Germany
All rights reserved.
English translation copyright © John Brownjohn 2008

This English translation first published in Great Britain in 2008 by
Haus Publishing Limited

This paperback edition published in 2011 by
The Armchair Traveller
at the bookHaus
70 Cadogan Place
London SW1X 9AH
www.thearmchairtraveller.com

The moral rights of the author have been asserted.

A CIP catalogue record for this book is available from the British Library

ISBN 978-1-906598-87-7

Typeset in Garamond by MacGuru Ltd
info@macguru.org.uk
Printed and bound in the UK by CPI Mackays, Chatham ME5 8TD

Contents

Foreword

This book is by way of being the epilogue to two previous publications of mine: *Napoleon. Verbannung und Verklärung* (Napoleon. Exile and Transfiguration), published in 2000, and my biography of Napoleon, which appeared in the spring of 2005. Even though St Helena, which I visited during the summer of 2000, is central to this account as well, its perspective is inevitably dominated by Napoleon, who lived and died there after spending over five years in exile. This requires no explanation, for the island would long ago have lapsed into oblivion had it not been for his enforced presence there.

Were the islands of the world to be ranked in order of remoteness and inaccessibility, St Helena would undoubtedly come near the top of the list. Its place on a list of well-known islands would be just as prominent. Taken together, these two statements add up to an undoubted paradox: St Helena, the world's best-known, least-known island.

A paradox of this kind presents an irresistible temptation to anyone whose wanderlust has not been completely quelled by advancing years. Nor will the visitor be disappointed, for the sheer adventurousness of his long voyage to the island will compensate him for much of what his imagination has led him to expect, but which is not altogether fulfilled by the reality of what he finds there. A part of 'the sad tropics', as the French ethnologist Claude Lévi-Strauss so aptly phrased it, St Helena is one of those earthly paradises which were damaged and deprived of their original character purely because the shadow of man fell across them. In St

Helena's case, this occurred over half a millennium ago. Nevertheless, it has preserved far more of its pristine appearance than many other 'dream islands', especially those that have been developed for purposes of tourism.

Discounting any spurious displays of 'folklore', most tropical islands are bereft of a surviving indigenous culture. Particularly when situated close to the stamping grounds of modern tourism, they prove to be palm-fringed, duty-free outposts of modern civilization. St Helena is different, though not in the sense that it possesses a culture of its own. Nevertheless, nowhere on the island will visitors encounter any of the obligatory tourist trash which Western culture, falsely guaranteeing that its ostentatious display certifies the wearer's good taste and distinction, has turned into an internationally successful export trade. To this extent, St Helena is a thoroughly old-fashioned place, a remote and bizarre vanishing point devoid of blaring discotheques and exempt from the risk of liver damage occasioned by the consumption of exotic cocktails. In short, St Helena is a philosophy of life. That is at once the great advantage and disadvantage of this singular island, with its kind and friendly inhabitants, which Napoleon abhorred primarily because it sentenced him to a fate he had always successfully avoided hitherto: a quiet life in a fixed abode.

Paris, July 2006

1

Arrival

There are countless descriptions of St Helena in existence. Those who are familiar with them will imagine themselves prepared for the worst. Just a dark speck on the horizon to begin with, the island gradually takes on shape and substance. The closer the ship gets, the more details show up and the more St Helena takes on the appearance of a rugged, dark brown mass which seamen, with their rough-hewn realism, have likened to a wart – an unlovely simile but extremely apt, for when seen from several miles away this tectonic outcrop really does resemble a blemish on the ocean's smooth epidermis. If one passed the island at this range, the sight of it would soon be eclipsed by that of the next school of dolphins gracefully escorting the ship on her way. But St Helena is the destination towards which the sturdy mailboat ploughs steadily through the long, rolling swell of the South Atlantic. As it draws nearer, the island looms up ever more forbiddingly and menacingly before the beholder's eye. No other island presents such an appearance. This is no enchanted isle off which the globe-trotter would wish to anchor, no dreamy South Pacific island with wide sandy beaches and green, palm-swathed hills that hold out the bogus promise of an earthly paradise. St Helena is the diametrical opposite of all that; it looks like a stage set for Hell.

Jutting straight out of the sea, dark, serrated, jagged masses of rock hundreds of metres high seem to echo, in every language living or dead, the announcement above the gate in Dante's *Inferno*: '*Lasciate ogni speranza voi qu'entrate*' – 'All hope abandon, ye who enter here!' One's first sight of the island is nothing less than frighteningly dramatic. It is consistent with this that the ship drops anchor far enough from the rocky shore for the truly awe-inspiring scenery to present passengers with a panorama of overwhelming unity. Far from being the work of some diabolical stage designer, however, this stems solely from the fact that St Helena possesses no harbour. Thanks to the powerful Atlantic swell, ships have to anchor in the roads and passengers are conveyed ashore by tender. This always holds out the prospect of a spectacle fraught with malicious amusement – one the islanders are reluctant to miss. In April 1984, when the governor had donned his white full-dress uniform in readiness to welcome Prince Andrew at the foot of the steep, slimy, seaweed-coated steps onto which visitors leap nimbly ashore to terra firma, he slipped and fell in. To have seen his pith helmet bobbing on the waves, its white ostrich feathers reminiscent of some rich exotic bloom, was an experience the islanders still relish to this day.

From this one can gain some idea of the abundant source of island gossip provided by the man who landed on St Helena on 15 October 1815, accompanied by a large retinue, and lived there in exile until his death on the afternoon of 5 May 1821. Lost amid the watery wastes of the South Atlantic, the little island was transformed by Napoleon's arrival into a stage for the performance of a play watched with curiosity and trepidation by the entire world. Strangely enough, however, the sensation created by that spectacle has long since subsided there, and memories of it are remarkably dim. In Jamestown, the island's 'capital', a small town wedged in a gorge between two steep, rocky hillsides, only one street name testifies to the erstwhile presence of the famous 'visitor', as the locals still call him. One looks in vain in Main Street's few shops for relevant souvenirs – mugs, plates or vases, ashtrays, glasses or trashy postcards bearing the man's celebrated likeness. It quickly becomes apparent that the islanders attach far more importance to other matters. One such was the visit of the American Joshua Slocum, the first man to circumnavigate the globe single-handed, who put in at St Helena on 14 April 1898 and spent several days there, as recorded by a plaque in the garden in front of the public library. Another was the rockfall that killed nine islanders in the middle of Jamestown in April 1890. 'IN MEMORY OF NINE PERSONS KILLED BY THE FALL OF 1500 TONS OF ROCK', as it says on the fountain erected in the victims' memory. (One wonders who estimated, let alone accurately measured, the weight of the said rockfall.)

No, Jamestown contains no memento of Napoleon apart from a street named after him. By contrast, one of the two guesthouses on Main Street bears the name of his vanquisher at Waterloo, the Duke of Wellington, who spent three weeks on St Helena in June 1805, on his way home from India. Sir Arthur Wellesley, as he then was, stated that the interior of the island was beautiful, and that the climate seemed to him to be the healthiest he had ever encountered. It was this impression of St Helena that settled Napoleon's ultimate fate after his fall from absolute power. Wellington's advice clinched the decision to banish Napoleon to the island for the rest of his life. He was far from alone in his favourable opinion of its climate and scenery. It was shared not only by all who lived on St Helena for considerable periods before the French Emperor, but by those who stayed there after him, for instance Charles Darwin, who visited the place in July 1836 and was reminded by its topography and vegetation of England or Wales. Governor R A Sterndale was particularly enthusiastic. Writing in 1902, he declared that St Helena's climate was one of the best to be found anywhere in the world. He even preferred it to that of Madeira, parts of it being drier. If only the island were more accessible and better known, he went on, it would make an ideal holiday resort for 'invalids and artists', who would gladly reside there for the sake of their health and the beautiful scenery.

It was Napoleon's special misfortune that, despite his many other attributes, he did not possess the makings of an artist. The place to which his vanquishers had chosen to exile him must have seemed final proof of the perfidy of Albion, his lifelong foe. One indication of this is that, to the surprise and disappointment of those who were only waiting for him to exclaim in horror and display some sign of consternation on that day in

October 1815, he remained silent when, after seventy-two days at sea, he watched the towering, bizarre-looking rocky island draw steadily nearer. Standing on the deck of the *Northumberland* surrounded by companions who, like him, were staring through telescopes or with the naked eye at the cloud-capped crags of the open-air stage on which they were to perform, Napoleon uttered not a word. And indeed, what *could* he have said, given that a single glance must have told him, of all men, that this island with the deceptively friendly name resembled an impregnable fortress? His military renown derived largely from this lightning ability to apprehend a situation and assess the strategic advantages of terrain. He now grasped the disastrous nature of his future fate: St Helena, as a proverbial saying has it, is a place 'with only one entrance and no exit'.

Chateaubriand was so puzzled by Napoleon's steadfast silence that he drew on his literary imagination in seeking to describe the Emperor's first impressions: 'He beheld the little town of Saint-James [Jamestown], which is wedged between jagged rocks; not a crack in this monotonous façade could be seen from which a cannon's maw did not peep forth. So much so that there seemed to be a wish to give the prisoner a welcome befitting his genius.' A pretty description, and apart from the cannon, which were never used and have all disappeared save the two that martially flank the entrance to the Castle in Jamestown's main square, the scene is much as it was when Napoleon first set eyes on it. The appearance of the island fortress, which Chateaubriand, who never visited it, aptly described as a 'rocky catafalque', has scarcely changed in the almost two centuries that have elapsed since then. Time, too, stands still at the ends of the earth.

That impression was not repudiated, even officially, by the governor, whom I called on at the Castle, his official seat, the day after I arrived. It went without saying, he told me, that the standard attributes of modern civilization – electricity, telephones, satellite television – had reached St Helena long ago. Discounting the tall radio mast in the vicinity of The Briars, however, neither the appearance of the island nor Jamestown itself had undergone any great changes. It was probable, therefore, that motor cars (finding a parking space in Main Street could often be difficult) were all that marred the scene familiar to Napoleon. However, his eye might have been caught by two architectural innovations: a handsome, ultra-marine building erected six years after his death in the main square beside St James's Church; and the precipitous flight of 699 steps leading up to Ladder Hill, a ridge some 200 metres high, which flanks Jamestown on the right-hand or western side.

Both structures are notable for their positively heroic futility. The smart blue building has functioned since its erection as the island's jail. As for the flight of steps known as 'Jacob's Ladder', on which work commenced in 1829, it served as a supply route to the fort on top of Ladder Hill, the keystone of the defences designed to protect Jamestown from attackers who never materialized. To that end, iron rails were laid on either side of the steps. On these, small wagons laden with supplies from the town could be hauled up the hillside by means of winches. The builder of this ingenious contrivance – with which St Helena, of all places, entered upon the railway era at a very early stage – was an artillery lieutenant named G W Melliss. Although Napoleon would doubtless have congratulated his fellow gunner on this feat, it was soon rendered redundant by the con-struction of a switchback road that zigzags up the hillside. All that now remains, therefore, is the flight of steps. Their gradient is so extreme – as much as 44 degrees in places – that, if you stand at the bottom and survey their full extent, you succumb to the alarming optical illusion that they are canting outwards and threatening to collapse on top of you. Once a year these steps form the venue for a contest in which the young people of the island take part. The winner is the one who manages to cover all 270 metres in the shortest time. I was assured that the existing record, which was set in 1990, stands at 5 minutes 28 seconds. Having no wish to compete myself, I was unsportsmanlike enough to take a taxi to the top and return to Jamestown on foot. Even the descent took me a good 15 minutes, and I arrived at the bottom of the steps with trembling knees and aching legs. It may be added that Ladder Hill had acquired its name before anyone thought of hewing steps into its precipitous basalt flanks.

Inaugurating them in 1832, the then governor expressed his confidence that the inhabitants of St Helena would soon become the most athletic people in the world. Their muscles and sinews would be toughened to such an extent that it would be easy for them to make their way across the mountains and hills with the utmost speed should it ever prove necessary to defend the island against invaders.

The island's jail, hemmed in by empty warehouses in the immediate vicinity of Jacob's Ladder, has been redundant ever since it was built, for the whole island constitutes a high security prison 122 square kilometres in extent. Beyond it lies an indifferent, seemingly infinite expanse of ocean. St Helena is over 1,800 kilometres from the nearest point on the coast of West Africa and over 3,500 kilometres from Brazil. It is probable that the jail was built merely because it completed the ensemble of public buildings enclosing the Parade, Jamestown's main square: the governor's official seat, the offices of the council responsible for the island's civil administration, the courthouse, the police station, and the public library, which was founded in 1813. The last to be erected in 1827, the jail completed the trinity on which Britain's colonial rule was based throughout her empire: administration, education and the threat of punishment. This is all the more remarkable because the island was then still owned by the East India Company and did not acquire the status of a Crown colony until April 1834. St Helena was subordinated to the Crown only temporarily, for the duration of Napoleon's exile, because the East India Company could not be expected to meet the additional expense. British taxpayers had to foot the bill for stationing the extra troops and naval units required to guard the island and its illustrious captive.

The jail was usually empty, the governor told me. There was almost no crime on St Helena, he said, this being a tradition of which the islanders could feel justly proud. All that marred this truly exemplary record was a growing but only statistically perceptible increase in road traffic offences, whose predominant cause was drink-driving. Fortunately, however, personal injury was the exception. One curious feature of the island's penal system was an 18th-century ordinance under which those found guilty of

6

malicious gossip were sentenced to be flogged in public. According to the governor, the wording of this ordinance did not apply to men. It had not, of course, been enforced for many years, just as there could be no real talk of a thoroughgoing penal system on the island. If someone was actually sentenced to a term of imprisonment, this merely meant that he was locked up in a cell at nightfall but could move freely throughout the island by day. In 1994 a Dutch sea captain sentenced to several years' imprisonment for drug smuggling had taken advantage of this lenient practice and cheated the law by fleeing to Brazil. He was the only person to succeed in escaping from the island, whereas attempts to escape on the part of Boer prisoners of war, several thousand of whom were interned on St Helena at the beginning of the 20th century, failed without exception. The runaways were thereafter condemned to spend the rest of their captivity in jail.

Like most colonial outposts in the tropics, Jamestown has been endowed by its past with an appearance of picturesque banality. The neat buildings on Main Street with their white or bright blue paintwork, cast-iron columns and dainty-looking balconies, exude a thoroughly melancholy aura that quickly proves to be an empty promise. No secret lurks behind those façades – not even an unpleasant exotic surprise. This end of the earth flaunts no surprises; at most, it displays bustling stagnation and a strangely antiquated vitality. Everything here that speaks of the present wears the undistinguished patina of long-forgotten familiarity, like pieces of furniture that strike you as modern in your youth, but, for that very reason, become little more appreciated as your yourself grow older. The interior decoration of my hotel accentuated this feeling in a way that made me wonder whether I was awake or dreaming. My attempts to resolve that uncertainty left me even more confused, however, because the rooms available to guests contained no television set whose news and images from the other, real world might have dispelled the persistent illusion that I was in a time warp, and that my arrival in St Helena had taken me back to the 1960s. All that promised to dispel my doubts on that score was a well-stocked bookcase. In addition to numerous English thrillers – all of which, when dipped into, proved to have been published in the

1950s – it contained two rows of well-thumbed *Readers Digests*. However, the most recent of those magazines was dated October 1962.

The governor merely laughed when I told him of my strange sense of disjunction from the present. That, he assured me, was a phenomenon frequently experienced by new arrivals and visitors to the island. He himself had felt no different on taking up his post some two years earlier – indeed, he had sometimes succumbed to the delusion that he was back in the 19th century. It was primarily a function of one's surroundings. The interior decoration of the Castle, his official seat, dated largely from the 19th century. Still more deceptive in that respect was Plantation House, the gubernatorial residence set in spacious old grounds. That its reception rooms, in particular, were furnished with such remarkable purity in the Georgian style was probably a tribute both to HM Government's notorious thrift and his predecessors' conservative taste. Even the two old giant tortoises in his grounds dated from that period and had already been there – or so legend had it – at the time of Napoleon's captivity.

Since he himself had mentioned the name of the man with whose fate St Helena is so indissolubly linked, I expressed surprise that Napoleon's memory was not cultivated more assiduously on the island. That was not altogether true, the governor replied, because both of the exile's former residences, The Briars and Longwood House, were owned by the French Republic, and so was his erstwhile grave in Geranium Valley. All these memorial sites were open to the public and maintained by a French consul who resided in Longwood House itself. Although Louis Philippe's government had arranged for Napoleon's mortal remains to be transferred to Paris in 1840, Longwood House had not been acquired from the British Crown until 1858. It was the great man's nephew, Napoleon III, who finally, after protracted negotiations, succeeded in purchasing his famous uncle's last residence for the very considerable sum of 178,565 gold francs.

That sum represented at least a symbolic indemnity for the substantial expenses Britain had incurred in lodging and guarding the exile for a total of sixty-eight months. It was a great deal of money to pay for a building used as a stable – one whose subsequent renovation and maintenance

8

would also cost the French government substantial sums – although the site of the empty grave, which was privately owned, was included in the deal. The Briars, the idyllically situated residence of the Balcombe family, where Napoleon stayed until mid-December 1815, was not bequeathed to the French state by descendants of that family until 1959.

In other words, although the governor was far too diplomatic to say so outright, the cultivation of Napoleon's memory on St Helena is an exclusively French preserve. In the British version of the island's history, the defeated Emperor's enforced presence plays only a very subordinate role, as witness E L Jackson's standard work published in 1903. Nevertheless, in the minds of today's islanders Napoleon continues to be a kind of villainous reference point. This was documented in 1990 by the *Saint Helena Herald*, the local daily, which reported the arrest of the aforesaid Dutchman for drug smuggling beneath the following front-page headline: 'The biggest affair in St Helena since Napoleon.' A somewhat bold assertion, for what would even five tons of marijuana signify compared to a man like Napoleon? Even so, it may be surmised that 'Boney' is still familiar to older islanders, at least, as a bogeyman of whom they may have heard stories in childhood like that told to six-year-old William Makepeace Thackeray, who caught a distant glimpse of the fallen Emperor while staying in St Helena with his family on the way home to England from India. He later recalled a black servant assuring him that 'that man over there' devoured three sheep a day and all the little children he could lay hands on.

But it wasn't altogether true, the governor told me, that Napoleon's sojourn on the island was totally ignored by the British – in fact I could see evidence of this in his office at the Castle. The mischievous glint in his eyes as he said this should have given me some indication of what I would now see: a framed lithograph of the ex-Emperor's nephew, Napoleon III, which adorns the wall behind his desk alongside a big Curnow Shipping calendar. The portrait was a gift from ex-Empress Eugénie, who had called in at St Helena in mid-July 1880, on her way back from South Africa after visiting the grave of her only son, a victim of the Zulu War. Writing to a woman friend at the time, she pointed out that she was the only bearer of Napoleon I's illustrious name to have visited the place where he languished and died.

This visit from Napoleon III's widow, who had been living in exile in England, provided St Helena with an enduring topic of conversation, but only because the island's dignitaries had been able to marvel at 'that greatest of all modern Sciences, the Electric Light' in the saloon of her steamship, the *Trojan*. This technological boon did not reach St Helena itself for over two generations. Not until the island was temporarily utilized for military purposes during the Second World War did it acquire a telephone and electricity network, which was initially supplied with power by the diesel generators of a submarine observation post installed at Longwood, of all places.

Napoleon spent only one night in Jamestown after his arrival. He slept at the home of Mr Henry Porteous, superintendent of the East India Company's gardens, which used to stand at the mouth of Main Street. Like most of the local buildings including the Castle, the original house fell prey to termites, which destroyed all its timbers and caused the walls and ceilings to collapse. Thus, with the exception of the Anglican church, which dates from 1774, the historical townscape, as Napoleon saw it, is largely a later reconstruction. Hence the cast-iron columns supporting the balconies, whose balustrades bear a more than fortuitous resemblance to rails. Thanks to the transport system devised by Lieutenant Melliss to ensure that the fort on Ladder Hill was kept supplied, some welcome building materials were available for preserving the buildings on Main Street and neighbouring Market Street from the depredations of termites.

Although details of the scene are no longer authentic in the sense that a visitor can be certain that the defeated Emperor's eagle eye once rested on them, this does apply, and in full measure, to the look of the whole ensemble. Now as then, it is the two steep, dark basalt hillsides between which the little town lies wedged that invest it with the lilliputian, toylike appearance of a Potemkin village. Now as then, reality turns out to be an illusion – pure sham and make-believe. Especially lively on market days, the hustle and bustle of Main and Market Streets, with their blaring horns and jostling pedestrians, create an impression of brisk but largely idle activity. Diverse in shape and scent, the colourful abundance of tropical fruit, fish and other wares assumed by visitors to be the origin of all this activity soon proves illusive, and their high hopes swiftly give way to profound disappointment. The market stalls offer thoroughly meagre fare: potatoes, onions, sweet potatoes, ugly little bananas, shrivelled and almost tasteless apples, the odd few mangoes, crates of dried fish. It all reminds one of the so-called 'free farmers' markets' that used to be common in countries behind the Iron Curtain.

This melancholy state of affairs applies also to the grocery stores, whose window displays seem designed to present the beholder with as comprehensive a view of their wares as possible. Elaborate pyramids constructed of jars of jam, fish, meat and vegetables alternate with minarets of beer and lemonade cans. The shops selling household goods and hardware look more tempting because they are less assimilable at a glance. Their entire stock seems to be piled up against the windows like a wave about to break. Pots and pans and aluminium tableware mingle in promiscuous confusion with crude-looking implements such as pliers and files, hammers and axes, scissors and screwdrivers, all of which make a curiously archaic, museum-like impression. This derives from the fact that they hail from India, where they were probably forged and manufactured by hand.

A fellow passenger on the mailboat had sung the praises of St Helena's honey. I simply had to get some, I was told; it was the only local produce worth buying. This authoritative pronouncement might have put an immediate damper on my overly optimistic expectations of the marvels that awaited me in St Helena, because the woman who uttered it was the widow of a former governor. She was, 'thank goodness', paying her very last visit to this *ultima Thule*. No, not for the sake of the honey, but in order to fulfil her late husband's wish to be buried there – his urn was in her luggage. He had succumbed to a tragic accident while on leave in England. In the course of a walking tour, he had slipped and fallen over a cliff to his death.

The unmistakably ironic nature of this statement did not dawn on me until I had become reasonably familiar with the island's topography. Although there were plenty of cliffs from which one could have fallen to one's death, this abundance did not extend to the island's famous honey, none of which could be found in any of Jamestown's shops. No, I was informed, it was a long time since they had stocked any St Helena honey. The island's bees produced too little of it, possibly because they were carried out to sea by the unremitting strength of the trade winds.

That explanation would undoubtedly have struck a chord with Napoleon and his companions, who found those winds a sore trial.

All who live on the island are accustomed to hardship. The Royal Mail Ship (RMS) *St Helena* provides their only regular contact with the rest of the world, primarily Britain and South Africa. If the vessel is late arriving, toothpaste, canned beer, cigarettes, salt and cooking oil can soon run short, in which case the islanders have to cope by going without. A paradise is supposed to possess a superabundance of everything, but it is so long since that state of affairs prevailed that no one, even on St Helena, can remember it.

2

'Sainte-Hélène, petite île…'

Perceptions of St Helena possess a history of their own. Roughly speaking, it may be divided into a 'before' and an 'after'. The former denotes the period since its discovery by Portuguese seafarers on 21 May 1502, the birthday of the eponymous saint and mother of Emperor Constantine the Great, whereas the latter began on 15 October 1815, when the *Northumberland*, with Napoleon and his entourage on board, dropped anchor off Jamestown. That was the day when international attention first focused itself on St Helena, and when accounts of the island, which were sparse and all too fanciful, became an object of sudden curiosity. Depending on one's admiration or contempt for the man who had been banished there, St Helena was depicted as an earthly paradise or a hell on earth. Napoleon's well-wishers perceived his place of exile as final evidence of Albion's perfidy and his enemies' implacable thirst for revenge. They had sentenced him to spend the rest of his days in that remote and exceedingly inhospitable place purely to be able to torture him to death without interference. That was a view which Napoleon and his companions vigorously promoted, and which Bonapartist propaganda and French historians favourable to the Emperor have never tired of advancing to this day.

Based primarily on the evidence of the 'gospels' written by Napoleon's disciples, who witnessed at least part of his almost five years of torment on the Golgotha in the South Atlantic, this Passion story has long since become fused into an indissoluble tangle of truth and fiction, propaganda and calumny. Irrespective of its numerous inconsistencies and patent contradictions, and of the demonstrably far from disinterested and impartial attitude of the protagonist and his leading 'evangelists', this argument has held undisputed sway ever since. Here we can discern Napoleon's last, decisive and uncharacteristically bloodless victory. The circumstances surrounding his exile and death on St Helena lent the myth in which his life came to fruition an apotheosis that will never fade for as long as his fame and legacy remain a bone of contention in people's memories. Heinrich Heine was one of the first to recognize this in his *Buch Le Grand*: 'And St Helena is the sacred grave to which the peoples of the East and West made pilgrimage in colourfully-beflagged ships, heartening themselves with grand memories of the deeds of the earthly Saviour who suffered under Hudson Lowe, as it is written in the gospels of Las Cases, O'Meara and Antommarchi.'

This debate was very largely stage-managed by Napoleon himself. It opened when he surprised all his companions by greeting the first sight of his island prison, which presents a truly awe-inspiring appearance, especially from the north, in silence. In so doing he displayed cool calculation as well as stoical resignation. That, and not naivety, which was alien to him in any case, is equally apparent from his first comment on St Helena, uttered the day after his arrival. Probably at the insistence of one of his companions, General Gourgaud, who wanted to insert the exile's first pronouncement on his future milieu, like some rare butterfly, among the hitherto trivial entries in his journal, Napoleon was prevailed on to remark, with a sigh: 'This is an unlovely place. I would have done better to remain in Egypt. I should now be Emperor of the whole of the Orient.'

This absurdly puerile-sounding expression of regret, which called his life's entire success story into question, is no less revealing of his true intentions. It had been his personal decision to sneak out of Cairo in the summer of 1799 and desert his doomed army, which he alone had embroiled in a pointless sand-table exercise, in order to seize power by means of a *coup d'état*. His contemptible flight from Egypt was the first, decisive step towards the greatness and folly whose bedazzlement rendered his downfall inevitable. After Waterloo, if not before, even Napoleon began to grasp that luck and skill cannot prevail indefinitely over the iron law that numerical superiority will win the day. His enemies could have summarily executed him. Blücher, who was not alone in recommending such a course of action, would have had him shot in cold blood over the grave of the Duc d'Enghien at Vincennes. Napoleon knew this, which was why he fled westwards to the coast. It seems doubtful that he really intended to escape to America, even though many of the moves he made at Fontainebleau point in that direction. That plan might even have been successful if boldly executed, but Napoleon vacillated, wasting precious days on futile démarches. His entourage gained the impression that he was no longer himself, and that misfortune – his sudden loss of power and fall from giddy heights – had robbed him of a sense of reality. This is far from impossible. At all events, his staff now ventured to do what they had always avoided doing: they bombarded him with well-meant advice and urged him to flee. By 3 July 1815, when he got to Rochefort on the Atlantic coast, the British fleet was blockading all the French ports. This precluded any attempt to escape to America undetected. The trap into which Napoleon's incomprehensible vacillation had manoeuvred him was now bound to close. Given his increasingly hopeless predicament, the confusion that reigned during those dramatic few days conveys an impression of frantic inertia. All at once, the erstwhile hunter whose dynamism had contributed so much to his success had become a hunted creature whose reflexes and instincts seemed to have become paralysed.

All evidence to the contrary, however, there is much to suggest that Napoleon still, even now, retained a firm hold on the threads of his destiny. Even at Rochefort, whence lurking British warships could be seen with the naked eye, he sought to convince his companions of his steadfast intention to escape. Although this smacked of a bad farce, Napoleon had been aware from the first of his great historical role. He could not afford to botch it by simply evading his responsibility. If the attempt failed, he would irretrievably discredit the reputation and renown no victor could rival. Even if it succeeded, however, flight offered no salvation. Retirement in America, where his brother Joseph, ex-King of Naples and Spain, would reside after escaping from Bordeaux, was an unthinkable alternative from Napoleon's point of view. This is not contradicted by Chateaubriand's article in *Le Conservateur* of 17 November 1818, which has been cited so often that it is now – and has long been – regarded as an incontrovertible certainty: 'His [i.e. Napoleon's] mere presence on the Atlantic coast of America would have compelled Europe to deploy on the opposite shore.'

That fear haunted the Bourbons in particular, who had precariously re-established themselves on the throne of France and were having to contend with a major problem: how to contain the highly combustible dissatisfaction of Napoleon's officers and men, now on half pay. This generated a mood of uncertainty which was shared by the other powers, who felt that, even in defeat, Napoleon posed a great and imponderable threat. The magic of his name alone sufficed for that. Finally, should he succeed in escaping a second time, the consequences of such a humiliation were not to be underestimated. That this had to be prevented at all costs was explicitly laid down in a resolution passed at the Congress of Vienna on 13 March 1815, not only by the members of the wartime coalition against Napoleon, Austria, Russia, Prussia and Great Britain, but also by Spain, Portugal, France and Sweden. The said resolution declared 'Bonaparte' to be 'proscribed' and 'forfeit of the protection of any law'. As if that were not enough, it also stated 'that Napoleon Bonaparte has set himself outside civilization and society, that he is regarded and prosecuted as an enemy and disturber of world peace and, consequently, as a criminal'. This verdict was further reinforced by a document dated 25 March 1815, in which the members of the wartime alliance pledged themselves to do everything in their power to render Napoleon harmless for all time.

Napoleon must have been cognizant of both resolutions, from which he could infer that he would not this time be treated with the leniency that had guided the victorious powers after his first abdication in 1814. On that occasion he had been allowed to retain his imperial title and assigned the island of Elba, off the Ligurian coast, as his place of residence. Napoleon ruled his miniature empire for a bare ten months, from the beginning of May 1814 until his escape on 26 February 1815. In the meantime, he occupied himself by inspecting the island, carrying out an abundance of road and harbour improvement schemes, and reopening some abandoned marble quarries. He was also commander-in-chief of his own little army of 400 men, whom he sometimes paraded as an antidote to the boredom that constantly beset him. Admiral de Boinod, who had been sent him by his brother Joseph, acted as his inspector-general. Boinod did little to enrich the Emperor's social life because he was almost stone-deaf and unable to hear anything fainter than a bellow. This demonstrated his suitability for any form of employment, however, and shows that the ex-Emperor was not without a sense of humour.

Napoleon was almost forty-five years old when exiled to Elba. As its sovereign ruler, he presided over the destinies of the island and its 13,000-odd inhabitants. Only there did his own security guarantee that the victorious powers felt safe from him. To make doubly sure, France and Austria maintained a host of spies on the island, whereas the British confined themselves to appointing a commissioner of their own, Sir Neil Campbell, who performed his custodial duties in a gentlemanly manner and was on thoroughly friendly terms with Napoleon. While evincing respect for a vanquished foe, these arrangements were not only lenient but foolish, because they were wanting in psychology and could not fail to hurt Napoleon's pride in a way he found insufferable. As one who considered himself a reincarnation of Alexander or Julius Caesar, he could not permit himself to be thought of as a Sancho Panza who, having formerly ruled the world, was content to be 'the governor of an island'.

Besides, Elba was a false Arcadia. The longer he tolerated this existence as a ridiculous petty princeling, the more he vitiated his claims to greatness. It was that profoundly dismaying prospect, as well as the lunatic hope of defeating his numerically superior enemies at the second attempt, which prompted Napoleon to turn his back on the pernicious idyll of Elba and stake everything on another throw of the dice. However the venture turned out, it would release him from the self-destructive embarrassment of vegetating in enforced insignificance. That was how he ended up at Rochefort, the end of the line and point of no return. His fate now rested in the hands of the victorious powers alone. On 10 July, with a view to gauging their intentions, Napoleon sent one of his staff, Comte de Las Cases, aboard the British warship *Bellerophon* to negotiate. Her captain, Maitland, informed Las Cases that, although he did not know what arrangements the British government had in mind with regard to the person of Emperor Napoleon, his own country and France were still in a state of war. He could not, therefore, permit any ship to leave Rochefort.

Given the prevailing circumstances, that information was both logical and correct. Napoleon now had no choice but to entrust himself, for better or worse, to the protection of the British fleet. That there was still a plausible alternative – that a bold attempt to escape might not, even now, have been doomed from the outset – is a speculative theory based solely on the agitation and indecision of those who formed Napoleon's extremely diverse entourage: on the one hand, naval officers whose much-vaunted courage was eventually dispelled by the fear of being charged with high treason by the Bourbons; on the other, ambitious young Napoleonic hot-heads who argued in favour of escape at any cost. This agitated hubbub, which Napoleon failed to quell, continued for three whole days. At last, on 13 July, he decided not to make a decision. There can be no other interpretation of his instructions to Las Cases and General Lallemand, issued on the morning of 14 July, to negotiate with Maitland once more and request his unimpeded passage to America. Maitland firmly replied that he could not entertain such a request. On his own initiative, however, he offered to take the Emperor aboard *Bellerophon* and convey him to England. He confirmed this invitation in writing, but qualified it by stating that he could not guarantee what attitude would be taken to Napoleon by the British government. That, too, was nothing if not correct.

There is no doubt that Captain Maitland made himself abundantly clear. That he expressed himself in misleading and ambiguous language – that he even held out the prospect that Napoleon would be granted asylum in England – is an assertion that has been repeated like a mantra, especially by French authors, who allege that it demonstrates all the duplicity and treachery to which France has always been subjected by the British. Las Cases did, in fact, broach the possibility of asylum in England as an alternative to exile in America during his first parley with Maitland, but the latter neither replied in the affirmative nor held out any hopes on that score. The only bona fide evidence that can be adduced is a letter Napoleon wrote to the Prince Regent on the afternoon of 14 July, which he sent to Captain Maitland together with the information that he and his entourage wished to go aboard *Bellerophon* the next morning. It is unsurprising, and explicable with relative ease, that a letter by someone as understandably interested in his own fate as Napoleon could exert such a magical and lasting effect on the critical discernment of later generations of his compatriots. His brief missive is nothing less than a Racinesque masterpiece of French theatrical literature whose veracity is no greater than the ability of its flowery tone to bedazzle the reader:

> Royal Highness,
> A victim of the factions which divide my country, and of the enmity
> of the greatest powers in Europe, I have ended my political career and
> am approaching, like Themistocles, to settle down at the hearth of
> the British people. I place myself under the protection of their laws,
> which I request from Your Royal Highness, being the mightiest, most
> tenacious and generous of my foes.

This letter is a documentary key to Napoleon's subsequent strategy, which was to charge the British with mistreating their captive in a duplicitous, deceitful and exquisitely cruel manner, having previously lured him into surrendering by promising him a benevolent reception and a guarantee of asylum. Whether Napoleon was really naive enough to believe that the Prince Regent or the British cabinet would be influenced in their decisions by such histrionic asseverations is a moot point. What mattered to him was that, in writing the above letter, he had created a document that handsomely testified to the sincerity of his sentiments. Anyone who gave it no credence, or whose manner conveyed that he was thoroughly unimpressed by it, would not only be putting himself in the wrong but incurring full responsibility for having to justify his actions – which could only, of course, be reprehensible.

Needless to say, this eloquent piece of classical French theatre failed to sway the British cabinet in determining what was to be done with Napoleon. The decision to deport him to St Helena was swiftly taken. It was dictated wholly by considerations of security, this being guaranteed in large part by the island's isolated position. The prime minister, Lord Liverpool, detailed the reasons governing the choice of St Helena in a letter dated 20 July 1815 to Lord Castlereagh, his foreign secretary, who was then in Paris. There were several arguments against interning Napoleon in England, he wrote. For one thing, it could lead to interminable litigation; for another, there was a risk that public opinion would swing in his favour and turn him, within a few months, into a person assured of widespread sympathy. Finally, his presence in England, or in some other European country, could only be detrimental because it would tend to prolong the current turmoil in France. Thus, the cabinet had very quickly come to the conclusion that St Helena was the best place on earth in which to detain such a person. It possessed a fine fortress that could be assigned him as a residence. The prevailing climate was said to be exceptionally salubrious. What was more, the island possessed only one anchorage; if need be, ships belonging to other nations could easily be prevented from putting in there. In view of St Helena's exceedingly remote location, all attempts to escape would be doomed to failure from the outset. Moreover, it was to be expected that Napoleon himself, if resident so far away from Europe, would very soon be forgotten.

This indicates that the British government's existing state of knowledge about St Helena was very limited. Also eloquent of Lord Liverpool's ignorance was his belief that Napoleon would soon recede into oblivion in his distant place of exile. On 31 July, after the Allied representatives in Paris had approved the proposal that Britain alone should be entrusted with his safekeeping, he was formally acquainted with the decision to deport him to St Helena by two members of the British government. St

Helena enjoyed a healthy climate, they assured him. Furthermore, his geographical location would enable him to be treated with considerably greater leniency than would be possible in any other place, given the need for appropriate security measures.

From this announcement Napoleon could readily infer the principal reason for banishing him to St Helena: he was to live in isolation, removed as far as possible from Europe, his former base of operations. This would automatically ensure that he soon succumbed to oblivion and, thus, to the great and abiding danger of being effectively exiled once and for all. Napoleon was bound to oppose this measure with all his might, if only for reasons of self-esteem, out of regard for his reputation and the image of his person and achievements he wished to bequeath to historians of the future. The strategy he proposed to employ is already apparent from the terms in which he formally protested against the deportation order. Having placed himself in British hands of his own free will, he demanded that his rights as a guest be respected. Assurances had been given him in that regard. By going aboard a British vessel he had entrusted himself to the hospitality of the British people, just as he would have done by entering one of their towns. Ship or town, it made no difference. As for the island of St Helena, that was tantamount to a death sentence. Instead, let him be consigned to a country house thirty miles from any coast. A government commissioner could also be instructed to monitor his correspondence and report on his conduct. Under those circumstances he would enjoy a certain amount of freedom. On St Helena, however, he would not survive for three months. No, he flatly refused to go there.

Although neither Napoleon nor anyone in his entourage had the least notion of what St Helena was like, its name evoked a wide variety of reactions ranging from alarm to horror. Discounting his formal protest, Napoleon alone evinced no perceptible emotion. Apart from declaring several times, with positively childish obstinacy, that he refused to go to St Helena, he displayed the almost cheerful stoicism to which he steadfastly clung on reaching his craggy, forbidding destination. At Auxonne in 1789, by an ironical quirk of fate of which he himself can scarcely have been aware, Napoleon had studied Abbé Lacroix's *Géographie moderne* as a twenty-year-old gunnery lieutenant. The last entry in his notebook, the fruit of his perusal of that work, read: '*Sainte-Hélène, petit île...*' The three dots were added by a later hand, presumably to invest that jotting with the tragic dimension it acquired on 5 May 1821, when the *St Helena Records*, the island's official chronicle, reported that the only noteworthy event to have occurred that day was the death of 'General Bonaparte'.

Thanks to information gleaned from a captured British officer who had been temporarily stationed there, Napoleon had augmented his knowledge of St Helena since making that entry, at least as regards the rocky island's fortifications and its great strategic importance to Britain's trade with the East Indies. In a letter dated *7 vendémiaire an XIII* (29 September 1804) to the navy minister, Vice-Admiral Decrés, First Consul Bonaparte gave orders that the island be captured. An expeditionary force of 1,200–1,500 men under the command of Brigadier Reille should suffice for the task, he wrote, especially as the British were quite unprepared for such an undertaking. Its object would be to employ the French squadron operating off St Helena to inflict immense damage on British merchant shipping for a period of three or four months. But Napoleon had no luck with any of his ambitious naval operations. This one came to naught because his detailed orders never reached Decrés. On 8 October 1804, because Napoleon feared that they had come to the knowledge of the British, the navy minister received instructions from Trèves to call the whole venture off.

Even before Napoleon's exile, St Helena had been enshrouded in a myth whose stubborn refusal to fade may have stemmed solely from its remote location. From the time of its discovery until well into the 18th century, it was thought to be a veritable earthly paradise in which all the marvels of creation could be found in the most complete and harmonious profusion. That was probably why the Spanish Jesuit Baltasar Gracián chose it as the setting for *El Criticón*, his convoluted allegorical portrait of human life, which was published in the middle of the 17th century and translated into all the major European languages in quick succession. Gracián based his fanciful description of St Helena's topography and vegetation on the few early travellers' accounts in existence. These told of fig trees that blossomed and bore an abundance of fruit at the same time, and of dense orange and lemon groves to be found throughout the island in valleys watered by limpid streams. However, there was no reference to those and other marvels in the book by Johann Georg Forster, who accompanied Captain Cook on his second circumnavigation of the globe (1772–5) and visited St Helena in passing. Forster mentions only that the rugged mountains in the island's interior were densely wooded to the very top. He also extols the prolific peach trees, whose fruit were 'excellent in flavour and differed from ours'. He expressly states, however, that no other kinds of fruit trees grew there, nor did grapes. 'Cabbages and other garden plants occur, but most of them are eaten by caterpillars.' Barley and wheat had been sown at one or two places on the island, but were destroyed by rats, 'countless numbers of which are to be found here'.

Forster's few remarks testify to an ecological disaster, for peach trees and cabbages, partridges and pheasants were not alone in not being indigenous to St Helena; so were rats, caterpillars and wild goats, which consequently had no natural enemies that might have kept their numbers down. Rats, in particular, which had been brought from Europe by the ships that put in there, became an absolute pest and took a long time to bring under control. They would even attack people and horses in their sleep, as Napoleon's companions occasionally discovered to their cost. Earlier horror stories, which spoke of big rats' nests in treetops, are also quite credible.

It was the voracious plague of rats, too, that is said to have given rise to the cultivation of yams from Madagascar, which were spurned by the rodents because of their bitter taste when raw but became a staple food, mainly of negro slaves and the poorer inhabitants of St Helena. We are told, however, that this speeded up the deforestation of the thickly wooded island, because yams, which are rich in starch, have to be boiled for hours to render them edible. But the consumption of timber for distillation purposes may have been no less deleterious, many of the islanders being so addicted to alcohol that the authorities had to take drastic measures to enforce temperance. Finally, the regeneration of wooded areas was inhibited by the wild goats that had been released on St Helena to provide seamen going ashore there with a convenient source of fresh meat. Over the years these goats had multiplied into huge herds, and no serious attempt to cull them was made until their ravages were almost irreparable, wind and rain having carried away the loose soil and exposed the bare rock beneath.

The rate at which these and other factors were destroying St Helena's once luxuriant vegetation emerges from a report by Francis Duncan, a British doctor who spent a considerable time on the island at the beginning of the 19th century. His account, published in London in 1805, stated that few of the peach trees extolled by Forster, formerly the island's most widespread fruit tree, were still to be found there. Peaches had once been so abundant that it was quite common to feed them to pigs. In the previous thirty years or so, however, nearly all the peach trees had been destroyed by an insect imported with vines from the Cape.

What completed this picture of an ecological disaster was the appearance in 1846 of 'white ants', or termites, which came to St Helena from Brazil in a slave ship captured by the Royal Navy. In addition to the slaves, who were released from their chains and interned in Rupert's Valley while awaiting trans-shipment to the West Indies, the vessel carried a cargo of timber infested – not that anyone knew it – with termites. That was how they reached the island. The mischief remained undetected until the first of Jamestown's buildings collapsed without warning and half of the books in the library had been ground to dust. One example of the insects' silent depredations is still recounted with glee by the islanders. A policeman suddenly noticed that a tree in full bloom in the gardens adjoining the Grand Parade had begun to sway like a drunk, then crashed to the ground. Being too poor to afford termite-resistant tropical hardwood, the islanders used rails to support the roofs of their rebuilt houses. Most of these came from the wrecks of ships driven onto the rocks by a storm while in transit from Britain to India.

The termite plague, whose full extent became apparent in the late

1850s, was the greatest disaster the islanders had had to contend with hitherto. The endemic hardships from which St Helena, the onetime paradise on earth, was suffering at that time are alluded to by Eugène François Masselin, an engineer captain who arrived there in March 1859 and spent eighteen months renovating Longwood, Napoleon I's former residence, on the orders of Napoleon III: 'Negroes, mulattos and many of the white labourers subsist on nothing but rice all year round.'

This and other, similar accounts suggest that St Helena seemed like a Garden of Eden, if at all, to seamen afflicted with scurvy and seasickness. That temporary but stubbornly persistent illusion, which had largely lost any basis in fact by the latter part of the 18th century, faded in proportion as the island's natural resources were destroyed, not only by imported pests, but by wasteful exploitation on the part of its human inhabitants. But what decisively accelerated the transition from paradisal abundance to stark deprivation were two other factors which, although St Helena shares them with many other exotic islands with a colonial past, were particularly evident there. One of them was slavery, which survived on the island for as long as it was administered by the East India Company; that is to say, excluding the period of Napoleon's exile, until 1834.

Although St Helena never, at any stage in its settlement by Europeans, maintained a regular plantation economy, its extensive agricultural activities serving only to make the island's population self-sufficient, slavery was customary from the first. However, the importing of slaves was very soon subjected to severe restrictions dictated by the fear that they might come to outnumber the white population. At the same time, slavery had a disastrous effect on the islanders' work ethic.

But what mainly frustrated the islanders' initially promising attempts to develop a thriving horticultural economy, for which their climate, topography and soil provided ideal prerequisites, was St Helena's swiftly and steadily increasing importance as a maritime staging post. Before this revolutionary development, which did not commence until the last third of the 18th century, the inhabitants lived on their farmsteads in the interior, tilling the fertile soil and lending the island its paradisal appearance.

At that time, Jamestown was a sparsely inhabited bunch of wretched hovels clustered around the fort and the church. Not until a ship hove in sight did the settlers leave their scattered farms and hurry down to the harbour with wagonloads of fruit, vegetables and other produce, which they bartered for the tools and other manufactured goods they lacked. Ships were also a source of news, entertainment and a rudimentary social life – welcome distractions from the monotony of their everyday existence. With the growth of shipping, however, the islanders developed the habit of living in Jamestown throughout the year and earning a modest but adequate living by barter.

The result of this development was that any form of agriculture carried on with care and expertise largely ceased. When Governor Beatson took up his post in July 1808, he found himself obliged to state in a report to the East India Company that only some ninety acres of land were being used for growing potatoes and garden produce. The yields obtained from that area were far from sufficient even to meet the requirements of visiting ships, which were having to pay exorbitant prices for fresh fruit. The island's 3,600-odd inhabitants lived almost exclusively on the Company's stores, but the prices they paid for those foodstuffs – mainly rice and salt beef – amounted to only one-third, at most, of their production costs. The consequence of such management was that the value of imports required solely to sustain the population had risen from £51,030 in 1800 to £114,961 in 1808.

Beatson, who tried to remedy the situation by introducing a series of vigorous measures, was soon opposed by an indignant group of islanders who even threatened open rebellion. His initial attempts to expand agricultural production by laying down maximum prices and rigidly controlling them were at first boycotted by the producers, who preferred to let their potatoes rot or dump them in the sea rather than sell them for six shillings a bushel instead of ten or twelve. It was not until 1811 that Beatson succeeded in imposing maximum prices for potatoes, beef and mutton, chickens, turkeys and geese. But not even that made any long-term difference to the islanders' slipshod attitude to farming, which persists to this day.

What decisively encouraged the indigenous population's addiction to the delights of colonial dependence, which Governor Beatson ultimately failed to cure, was Napoleon's internment. According to a statistic dated September 1815, or just before his arrival, the resident population of the island numbered 2,876 souls. Of these, 776 were white, 1,358 slaves, 447 emancipated Africans, 280 Chinese, and 15 Indian indentured labourers. Add to these a garrison of over 1,000 men, and the island's total population increased to around 4,000. But that figure was suddenly more than doubled by the additional troops stationed on the island to guard Napoleon and the crews of the naval squadron on permanent patrol in the waters around it. One immediate effect of this was to boost the circulation of money, which consisted of a truly Babylonian diversity of gold, silver and copper coinage whose current value relative to the pound sterling was laid down by the island authorities. The commonest form of currency was the Indian 'star pagoda', but there were also Spanish doubloons, Maria Theresa thalers, Venetian sequins, rupees, German and Dutch gulden, and, last but not least, after the arrival of Napoleon and his retinue, an increased number of 'napoleons' and louis d'or.

A few examples may serve to illustrate the immense amount of money circulating on the island. The British taxpayer had to fork out £12,000 a year to defray the cost of Napoleon's household, which comprised thirty-eight persons. In addition, the exile and his companions possessed considerable sums of money of their own. The annual pay and expenses of the British governor, Napoleon's jailer-in-chief, amounted to another £12,000. Further substantial sums were swallowed up by the pay and rations of the additional troops stationed on the island to guard the prisoner. This population growth led to an exorbitant rise in the demand for foodstuffs and other consumer goods, which resulted in an import boom maintained by a steady increase in the number of merchantmen plying between St Helena and Britain or the Cape. The readily understandable result of all this was a rapid upsurge in prices for goods and services and, thus, a purely inflation-based increase in prosperity. Above all, however, the rapid rise in the demand for labour in the service sector, coupled with the relatively high wages paid by the military authorities to those who helped to keep their troops supplied, proved an immense boost to the rural exodus and ended by transforming hitherto sleepy little Jamestown into a kind of gold-rush town.

All manner of places of entertainment – even a theatre – were now established, and a modest form of social life came into being. Its focal point was the governor, who resided at Plantation House, and its supporting cast consisted of island bigwigs, senior British army officers, many of them accompanied by their wives, naval officers, dignitaries in transit with their families, and the more senior members of Napoleon's staff. It was characteristic of this period that it initiated an upsurge in the founding of clubs and charitable institutions which continued throughout the 19th century. The earliest of these institutions was the Benevolent Society, established in 1814. Curiously enough, three masonic lodges also flourished in St Helena. The mysterious Ancient Order of Foresters was founded in 1871, a fateful year from the island's point of view, given that the opening of the Suez Canal in 1869 had deprived St Helena of its lucrative monopoly of the shipping route between Europe and Asia. According to weather-worn but still legible inscriptions, all these associations continue to occupy their original premises in Jamestown.

After Napoleon's death and the withdrawal of most of the garrison and the naval squadron, the island's spurious prosperity soon began to fade. What blinded its inhabitants to the realization that they were living in an inescapable poverty trap was their strategically favourable maritime position, which held good for a considerable time. As long as hundreds of ships continued to drop anchor off Jamestown to supplement their stores and trade some of their cargoes in exchange, the islanders were guaranteed a certain degree of economic prosperity. In 1845, a record year, 1,458 vessels anchored in the roads off Jamestown; in 1948, a century later, only 31 did so. What accounted for this decline, apart from the Suez Canal, were advances in shipbuilding technology: because vessels became ever bigger and faster, they could dispense with an intermediate stop at St Helena to take on fresh water or coal. Today, only one ship constitutes the major maritime link between the island and the rest of the world: the RMS *St Helena*, which calls there four times a year.

This prior history explains why St Helena is more than ever dependent today on the mother country's substantial financial support. Of the ten territories that now constitute the rump of the formerly worldwide British Empire – Anguilla, the Bermudas, the Virgin Islands, the Cayman Islands, the Falklands, Gibraltar, Montserrat, Pitcairn and the Turks and Caicos Islands – only St Helena and its two administrative dependencies, Ascension and Tristan da Cunha, are dependent on yearly financial aid from London. Not only is well over 90 per cent of the island's budget financed by the British taxpayer, but the wages and salaries of around 80 per cent of the able-bodied population are paid out of public funds. Most of the remaining 20 per cent of 'Saints', as the islanders call themselves, work in the Falklands or on the big US-financed airfield and military base on Ascension, generally on two-year employment contracts. It is their largely tax-free income that underpins St Helena's modest level of prosperity. Apart from the exportation of labour, the island's other main source of income is the sale of its coveted postage stamps to collectors all over the world, which brings in some £10,000 annually.

For a long time, the 'Saints' had almost no chance of escaping from their remote island poverty trap because Margaret Thatcher's government had deprived them, like the inhabitants of other overseas territories administered by the Crown, of their British citizenship. As a result, they required a visa even to travel to Britain, their unwelcoming motherland, but visas were issued only to those who had a work permit and a job or a prepaid return ticket. This unjust regulation, which had been fiercely opposed by the Anglican bishop resident on the island, was revoked on 21 May 2002, to mark the 500th anniversary of the discovery of St Helena. Its consequences can be clearly inferred from the size of the island's population, which decreased from over 5,000 at the end of 1998 to 3,863 in July 2004. Another impediment to escaping from this prison, which still exists, is that St Helena, Ascension, Tristan da Cunha and the Falklands have a currency of their own. This is the St Helena pound, which enjoys parity with the pound sterling but is not freely convertible, as witness my unsuccessful attempt to change a St Helena £10 note on my return to Heathrow. In order to effect this transaction, I was referred to the Bank of England...

But the 'Saints' are unembittered by this. All the islanders I met were extremely friendly, open-minded individuals who assured me, promptly and without being asked, that they liked living on St Helena and preferred it to any other place on earth. Although far from sharing that sentiment, I had no reason to doubt their sincerity. Perhaps a state of not unduly perceptible collective poverty, coupled with the joys of colonial tutelage and freedom from the cares of existence, create a happiness hard to convey to outsiders.

One conspicuous symbol of that happiness is a red can inscribed 'Castle Beer'. The RMS *St Helena* transports tons of these cans to the island whenever she returns from South Africa, or 'the Cape', as it is still known locally. Some years ago, when the ship was immobilized by engine failure, the islanders were without beer and cigarettes for quite a while. Being able to grow tobacco and brew beer, they experimented with both activities, only to give up again. It is doubtless more convenient to import both these delights than to produce them by the sweat of one's brow. I was told that Jamestown had once boasted two breweries. They brewed excellent beer, apparently, but both went bankrupt because the 'Saints' were so impoverished that the draught ale went off before the barrels were even half empty. Although this story may be apocryphal, it is a melancholy fact that the mouths of the two bronze cannon flanking the gateway into the Castle, the governor's headquarters, are permanently choked with empty cans of 'Castle Beer'. The islanders' cup floweth over!

3

The Scene of the 'Crime'

Napoleon spent most of his sojourn on St Helena in two places: The Briars and Longwood House. Together, they form the setting for what is even now represented as a grandiose drama, the heroic struggle of one solitary but towering individual who defended himself to the last, and with rare dignity, against petty vindictiveness and the countless, senseless tribulations inflicted on him by a bunch of lilliputians whose sole intention was to kill him as slowly as they could. Forever retold, and not only by the French, the story of Napoleon's exile and death has become a *légende noire* that denigrates their neighbours across the Channel as 'perfidious Albion'. This is what invests both places with their positively mythical significance: they are the shrines of a cult that commemorates one of a proud nation's most important periods in history – one from which, even today, it derives much of its political self-assurance. Symbolic of this is the immaculate tricolour fluttering over Longwood in the trade wind.

Shrines need custodians and an influx of pilgrims. Without these, their aura begins to fade; they forfeit their acquired significance and degenerate into ordinary antiquities that attract a certain amount of attention, if at all, because of their impressive setting. This cannot be said of either The Briars or Longwood House. True believers are fascinated by them purely because they approach both places in the knowledge that HE lived, suffered and died there. A great abundance of information on the subject comes from numerous contemporaries who missed nothing and considered even the most trivial details worthy of record. Influenced by the most diverse temperaments, intellects and points of view, sympathies and antipathies, expectations and evaluations, such is the material basis of a body of scholarship that long ago took on the characteristics of a Napoleonic theology.

Those who approach these two places devoid of true faith and wholly ignorant of the sacred texts or their exegesis by their foremost interpreters – of whom there has been no lack in any succeeding French generation – will fail to feel the thrill that would turn their visit into an unforgettable experience. All that overcomes them is a fleeting sense of the attention-seeking insignificance characteristic of certain provincial museums whose meagre inventories are transfigured into a pedagogic virtue.

But the genuine pilgrim will undergo positively supernatural experiences there. Octave Aubry, for example, a member of the Académie Française who spent three months on St Helena in the early 1930s, wrote as follows in the foreword to his *Saint-Hélène*, which has since become a 'classic' work on the subject: 'I breathed the air he breathed, I saw his ghost, yes, I saw him get to his feet behind those unremarkable doors, in those mean rooms, saw him thrust his Austerlitz glass through the hole in his shutter and survey the distant tents of Deadwood Camp; I heard him speak, heard him unbosom himself to his last few faithful followers.'

Napoleon spent only one night in the sultry heat of Jamestown. While awaiting the completion of the extensions and alterations to Longwood House, the deputy governor's residence that had been assigned to him and his retinue, he moved at his own request into a pavilion or summerhouse belonging to The Briars, an idyllically situated country house occupied by an official of the East India Company, William Balcombe, and his family. All that survives of this bucolic oasis, then a group of buildings set in the midst of a well-kept garden, is that strangely incongruous-looking pavilion. It is closely hemmed in on three sides by an industrial wasteland, fenced off and overgrown with weeds, on which massive cable drums lie scattered around the foot of a tall radio mast. The site is owned by Cable & Wireless, whose local director used to be quartered in the former summerhouse – more precisely, in the playroom of the Balcombes' four children. The company has since moved to more accessible Ascension Island. This is why the building with the melancholy designation 'Exiles Club', which stands just behind the pavilion, and in which company employees presumably made vain attempts to dispel their boredom, is inexorably lapsing into decay.

Napoleon's two months at The Briars were probably the least unhappy period of his exile. The only members of his retinue permanently on hand there were his valet, Louis Marchand, and the Las Cases, father and son. Because this made it easier for him to discard the relentless constraints of court etiquette and the deliberately aloof manner he always cultivated on other occasions, he was able to take an active part in the Balcombes' affectionate and uncomplicated family life. That, at any rate, is how one of the Balcombe daughters, Betsy, describes it in her *Recollections of Napoleon at St Helena*, first published in 1844. We are told that the erstwhile god of war participated with surprising exuberance in all kinds of frolics, that he joined in games of blind man's buff, good-naturedly tolerated mimicry, and even, with tousled hair, savage grunts and menacing gesticulations, scared Betsy's little girlfriends with impersonations of the ferocious ogre he had always been portrayed to them as.

Historians of his exile have either cast mild doubt on the credibility of this cheerful intermezzo in the Napoleonic tale of woe or ignored it altogether. This is not surprising, for not even a figure like that of Simon of Cyrene can be fitted into the Manichaean system of that other Passion. But what surprises one most about Betsy's account is the question it inevitably poses: Would not the protagonist of the drama in progress on St Helena have been granted a happier lot had he dispensed with his motley, bloated retinue on the one hand, and, on the other, adopted an attitude in his misfortune that did not in any way betray his claim to respect but eschewed the sometimes brusque arrogance which merely betrayed the onetime Corsican gunnery lieutenant who had risen to become Emperor of the French? Napoleon was always conscious of this for as long as his star was in the ascendant, as many of his utterances demonstrate. Once married to a Habsburg princess in the person of Marie-Louise of Austria, however, he cherished the illusion that he was the equal by birth of other crowned heads, if not their superior. But they represented a claim that had long ago been destroyed by the French Revolution, to which he owed so much. Thus, as a historic and truly revolutionary exception, he lived a kind of lie in which he became increasingly entrenched the more his star waned to final extinction. One might infer that this was his real tragedy, a perception of which is obscured by the purely superficial circumstances of his exile, which attract sympathy although he himself was very largely responsible for them – a fact that is often ignored.

It is far from fortuitous, therefore, that The Briars should now be a Napoleonic cult site with a vaguely indeterminate, unassuming appearance. Not even the undemanding Napoleon-worshipper will be impressed by what the two-room museum has to offer: a cup from which he is alleged to have drunk and a faded scrap of the carpet that covered the floor during his stay. Preserved like a relic in a glass case, that pathetic object contrasts in a strangely derisory way with the neat, bright room in which it is displayed. But can this really be the room Napoleon entered for the first time on 18 October 1815? So much grandeur and tragedy in so small a compass? No, unable to feel reverence or profound emotion, the visitor shrugs and turns to go. Displayed in the museum's other, considerably smaller room are some engravings and lithographs and one or two drawings. Depictions of St Helena, The Briars and Napoleon himself, these long-familiar illustrations from the relevant literature have been assembled and laid out in order to fill a void that seems all the emptier for their presence. Napoleon 'doesn't live here any more', and his ghost refuses to be raised. Visible through the window are the cable drums and the steel latticework of the radio mast. Britannia rules the air waves. 'Perfidious Albion' is in evidence wherever one looks.

Oh yes, affixed to the entrance of The Briars museum is a metal plaque stating in French that a descendant of the Balcombe family bequeathed this historic building to the French Republic in 1959. Prior to that date, another plaque recorded in English that Sir Arthur Wellesley, later the

Duke of Wellington, had lodged there during his stay on the island between 21 June and 3 July 1805. He had previously spent his first night in the same Jamestown house as Napoleon. This is doubly remarkable. Great generals have an unerring eye for handsome buildings in idyllic surroundings, and secular cult sites lay claim to the same exclusivity as the Christian religion. Thus, The Briars' few visitors are kept uninformed about the curious coincidence that Wellington's and Napoleon's paths once crossed in this of all places.

Napoleon remained at The Briars while the alterations and additions to Longwood House were still in full swing. However, in contrast to his first exile on Elba, where he had taken an active interest in the renovation of his residence, the Palazzo Mulini, Napoleon now left it to members of his retinue to keep him informed of the progress of work on Longwood. No sooner was this approaching completion, however, than a problem arose – one to which inordinate space is devoted by Napoleonic hagiographers. Indeed, in *The Black Room at Longwood*, a French bestseller published in 1997 by the journalist Jean-Paul Kauffmann, it becomes the principal theme. Allegedly, the ex-Emperor's sense of smell was so hypersensitive that the fumes of fresh paint proved an unbearable strain on his nerves and injurious to his health. On 7 December 1815, Chamberlain Bertrand and Aide-de-Camp Gourgaud reported that, in view of the Emperor's sensitivity, Longwood's paintwork was still far too fresh to warrant his moving in. Similarly, Las Cases reported the next day that, although the smell of paint was very faint, he considered it far too strong for Napoleon's sensitive nose. Finally, after inspecting Longwood again, Bertrand was able to announce on 9 December that the paintwork had ceased to give off any noxious fumes, whereupon Napoleon commanded his entire household to move into their new residence the following day.

This incidental episode possesses a certain importance, but not the importance ascribed to it by Napoleonic hagiographers. On Elba Napoleon had raised no objections to taking up residence in the Palazzo Mulini while renovation work was still in progress – and that despite express warnings from his personal physician, Fourreau de Beauregard, who drew his attention to the noxious effluvium of fresh paint. Not only was he unworried by the smell, but he sometimes took an active part in the work by mixing fresh paint that adhered to his delicate hands. In view of this, the answer to this supposedly physiological enigma – why the patient's susceptibility to smells should have undergone a radical change from one island to another, from his first to his second place of exile – cannot lie in his particular physical constitution or pronounced sensitivity.

The origins of Longwood House, the largest and most imposing building on the island apart from Plantation House, the governor's residence, go back to the latter third of the 18th century. In 1787, Lieutenant-Governor Francis Robson built a single-storeyed house of seven rooms, annexed to which were some smaller servants' quarters, a kitchen, and an enclosed courtyard. The building's original nucleus was a cow-house which Robson integrated and divided into four rooms. This economy proved to be a grave deficiency affecting the whole complex. In order to avoid differences in level, the structural additions were neither provided with cellars nor raised on low supports that would have enabled the air to circulate beneath them – a desirable feature in view of the constant tropical humidity. Napoleon and his staff were to suffer badly from this architectural bodge-up, hence their fully justified complaints about the 'cellarlike' atmosphere that prevailed at Longwood all year round. Eugène François Masselin, the engineer captain who was sent to St Helena for two years in 1859 on instructions from Napoleon III to renovate the house from top to bottom, has left a drastic description of the consequences of the permanent humidity prevailing inside: 'Silks and gloves, even when kept tightly shut up in a chest, soon became coated with irremovable stains; leather was covered with a thick film of mildew within a few days.'

The original building, with its T-shaped ground plan, was swiftly and substantially enlarged to accommodate Napoleon and his household. Built on to the main entrance, which faced north, was a spacious, hall-like room measuring nine metres by six, the ceiling being almost four metres high. A timber structure, but the only one to repose on solid stone foundations, it has five large windows, three facing west and two east, the latter pair being separated by a fireplace. Thanks to these and to two smaller windows flanking the door that opens on to a terrace from which five stone steps lead down to the garden, the room makes an agreeably bright and cheerful impression. However, Napoleon always ensured that the curtains were tightly closed to prevent himself from being spied on from outside. Although the room differs from all the rest in never having been damp, thanks to its foundations, this habit of his plunged it in gloom and made it impossible to read or write there. The adjoining room, which was constructed of stone and had been built by Lieutenant-Governor Robson, served Napoleon as a drawing room and reception room for visitors. The camp bed on which he died on 5 May 1821 was set up in there during the final phase of his illness. The other rooms in the broad crosspiece of the T dated from Robson's day and were used by Napoleon as his dining room, library, living room and bedroom. Beyond the latter lay the bathroom containing the big zinc tub in which the exile spent so much time, together with his valet's room.

All these premises, which were used exclusively by Napoleon, were separated by a corridor, and by a courtyard enclosed on the south side by domestic offices and servants' quarters, from the much bigger architectural complex that housed all the rest of the staff except for Chamberlain Bertrand and his family. Including the kitchen, this comprised twenty-five rooms of widely differing sizes, most of which were built in a mere two months by carpenters and seamen from the *Northumberland*, who had to transport all the requisite building materials from Jamestown, some five miles distant. It was this rush that was to blame for the numerous shortcomings so bitterly complained of by the occupants of Longwood House.

These additional premises, which were still under construction when Napoleon moved into his new quarters, were simply huts roofed with wooden battens. To keep out the rain, the flimsy buildings were covered with roofing paper daubed with a mixture of tar and grit. However, strong sunlight melted this coating and dissolved the paper, with the result that rain soon seeped into the primitive rooms and became a source of constant complaints. But the occupants must have been even more sorely plagued by rats, which turned Longwood House into a veritable rodents' stronghold because it provided them with an ideal habitat as well as an abundance of food. The wooden partitions between the rooms were of double thickness to create a gap for ventilation, and rats could be heard scampering around day and night within these interstices and beneath the floorboards, which were not flush in many places because of the uneven ground. Even when patched with sheets of zinc, the numerous holes they gnawed in the walls enabled them to gain unobstructed access to the staff living quarters. On one occasion a plump rat is reported to have leapt out of Napoleon's hat, which he had left on a shelf.

All attempts to control this plague, which made it impossible to keep poultry because the rats not only helped themselves to eggs but devoured the hens themselves, came to nothing. The dogs and cats employed in all-out campaigns against the rodents were regularly overwhelmed by sheer numbers. One of these dogs, Sambo by name, hailed from China and had pale fur with brown spots. Taken back to France by Bertrand in 1821 and stuffed, its remains form one of the more bizarre attractions in the museum of Napoleonic memorabilia bequeathed by him to Châteauroux, his birthplace. Combating the plague with poison, on the other hand, seemed inadvisable because the corpses would have decayed inside the walls, where their stench would have rendered the premises uninhabitable.

Word of the plague of rats besetting Napoleon and his household reached Britain and spread throughout Europe, where it inspired numerous cartoons. One depicted the ex-Emperor reading out the *Acte conditionnel*, the liberal constitution he had promised the French people after his return from Elba, to a rodent assembly. Others showed him forming and training an army of rats; leading an imperial guard of cats into battle against them mounted on a goat; being waited on at table by liveried rats; sitting with them in a cellar and planning another invasion of France; languishing in a rat trap with the rodents performing a derisive dance around him; and, finally, taking refuge on the roof of his house, which seems to be adrift in an ocean of rats. Everyone kicks a man when he's down.

Nevertheless, although criticisms of the manifest architectural shortcomings of Longwood House were all too justified, an impartial visitor to the rooms at Napoleon's disposal will be unable to comprehend the persistent complaints that were also made about their allegedly cramped dimensions and inadequate furnishings. All of them, including the bathroom, are well-proportioned and quite spacious. The drawing room, for example, measures eight metres by five and has a ceiling height of almost four metres. There are two windows facing west and a fireplace in the wall opposite them. The dining room next door is very little smaller, measuring seven metres by five, and its ceiling is a good three metres high like that of all the remaining rooms. This room, too, has a fireplace and is lit by a french door leading into the garden. The next room to the east, the library, measures some six metres by five. It is excellently lit by two windows facing north and another french door leading into the garden. To the west of the dining room are two further rooms of almost equal size, each roughly five metres square, which functioned as Napoleon's study and bedroom.

I am not being pedantic in listing the dimensions of these rooms – far from it, for two comparisons may serve to show how exaggerated Napoleon's repeated complaints about them were. For his private, unofficial use, he had a definite preference for relatively small rooms where he could readily create the rather overheated atmosphere in which he felt particularly comfortable by shutting the windows and maintaining a good open fire. His bedroom at Malmaison, for instance, was very little bigger than the one he slept in at Longwood, whereas the study and bedroom he had specially built for himself at San Martino on Elba were even smaller.

Though certainly not luxurious, all these rooms were comfortably furnished, the walls being either panelled or cloth-lined. Generally speaking, therefore, Napoleon had at his disposal a quite spacious and comfortable residence. Apart from a few pictures, some silver candelabra, Frederick the Great's watch, which Napoleon had appropriated from Sanssouci as a spoil of war, and the big silver washbasin he had used at the Tuileries, all the other furnishings – tables, cupboards, *chaises-longues*, armchairs, upright chairs – were provided by the British government and continuously augmented, for instance by a large mahogany billiard table, which was set up in the entrance hall. All these practical and thoroughly tasteful appointments transformed Longwood House into a not overly lavish but pleasant retreat such as might have been afforded by a well-to-do gentleman of private means.

What endowed this country house with its special character, however, was its position on the Longwood plateau, from which the varied panorama presented by St Helena is visible on every side. Jagged, towering peaks alternate with deep valleys beyond which lie other dark green plateaux and, in the far distance, the deep blue Atlantic. The scenery is thoroughly impressive and, in its topographical diversity of shapes and colours, probably unique. Of course, this view may be dismissed merely as a naive or romantic transfiguration, for Longwood's highland plateau was admirably suited to the internment of Napoleon and his household on security grounds. The only access to it in those days was a far more tortuous but easily monitored road, and it was cut off from the rest of the island by precipitous rocky chasms, some of them several hundred metres deep.

But there are two ways of looking at anything, as we all know, and what one person finds fascinating and delightful will depress or bore another. As the poet Henri Amiel says, every landscape is a condition of the soul. That applies in very special measure to Longwood House, for any visitors to the property today, and above all any devotees of Napoleon, go there in awareness of the complaints and grievances of its onetime occupants. They will know of the harsh verdicts historians have passed on the petty behaviour and positively pathological mistrust displayed towards the exile and his entourage by Napoleon's jailers, Admiral Sir George Cockburn and, more especially, his best-hated successor, Sir Hudson Lowe. Those who view the scene of the drama through those spectacles will not only find corroboration of what they already knew; they will make it their ambition to discover new and hitherto insufficiently known or appreciated factors supportive of a drastic sentence passed long ago.

It is undoubtedly true that not all the complaints and reproaches levelled by its occupants at the condition and location of Longwood House, at the trade winds, the inescapable humidity and chill temperatures, can be repudiated out of hand. What renders them so unconvincing, on the other hand, is their monotony, their offensive, self-righteous, puffed-up vehemence, and the thoroughly rancorous language in which they were couched, orally or in writing. This was all a deliberate ploy, of course. The aim was to grind the British authorities down and induce them to enter into negotiations to which even greater exception could be taken. The occupants of Longwood House were all the more successful in this because their jailer for the majority of Napoleon's exile, Sir Hudson Lowe, was far from equal to his difficult task. At the same time, it seems quite remarkable that Napoleon, of all men, should have demanded that his treatment and accommodation conform to 'humanitarian standards' which he himself had loftily disregarded in comparable circumstances. Like his devotees, he was precluded from expressing any moral indignation about the allegedly cruel and unjust treatment he was undergoing, if only because of the disgraceful ruse with which, as First Consul, he engineered the capture of his erstwhile admirer and great opponent, Toussaint Louverture, the Haitian freedom fighter, who was imprisoned in a gloomy dungeon in the castle of Joux at Pontarlier, in the bleakest part of the Jura, and died a miserable death there.

Such indignation is doubly unjustified because Napoleon himself was largely responsible for having to live in the conditions he so vehemently complained of, for his sojourn at Longwood House was regarded, even in London, as nothing more than an unavoidable temporary solution. As early as August 1815, the British government commissioned the architect William Atkinson to produce, within six weeks, plans for a new residence on St Helena to be constructed as quickly as possible from prefabricated components. Both simple and logical, the plans envisaged the erection on stone foundations of an oak frame which could be speedily filled with stonework quarried on the island. The dimensions of this projected building are impressive in themselves: a single-storeyed mansion in the classical country house style, it was originally designed to have a total living area of 2,137 square metres. None of the twenty-four rooms intended for

Napoleon and his immediate staff measured less than 7.5 metres by 5, and seventeen of them were entrusted to George Bullock, then regarded as one of England's leading interior designers.

The materials for the elaborate timber structure and some of the interior fittings for Longwood New House, as the projected building was promptly named, reached St Helena by the beginning of May 1816, but work on it did not start until two years later. Why not? Governor Sir Hudson Lowe allowed himself to be swayed by Napoleon, whose attitude to the project varied between indifference and extreme scepticism. Not only did he describe it as a sheer waste of money, but he predicted – correctly, as it turned out – that he would be dead by the time the building was finished. So absolutely nothing happened for more than a year. Late in 1817, Lowe received instructions from London that he himself was to decide whether to erect a smaller house and use the surplus materials to enlarge Longwood Old House. The renewed state of indecision into which this plunged him lasted until August 1818, when London categorically instructed him to start work on the new building.

Once the original plans had been completely revised by Montholon, work on the foundations commenced at the beginning of September 1818. However, the elaborate internal structure and entire furnishing of what was by far the biggest architectural complex on the island were not completed until February 1821, by which time Napoleon was already in the throes of the rapid physical decline from which death released him on 5 May. But this seeming tragedy stemmed, in essence, from a deliberate policy for which Napoleon himself was chiefly responsible. From many points of view, Longwood Old House was just a temporary arrangement which created the illusion that he would not remain an exile to the end of his days. It also provided him with a welcome opportunity to complain of its many manifest shortcomings. His protests would have been defused once and for all by a move to Longwood New House. Therein lies the main reason why Napoleon stubbornly refused, from the very first, to take any interest his new abode, even though it would have offered him and his staff the very comforts whose absence they so loudly deplored. At the same time, his new surroundings would have seriously weakened the propaganda value of the martyrdom he was alleged to be undergoing on St Helena.

Even when Longwood New House was largely complete at the beginning of 1820, Napoleon still refused to move in. His main objection now was a low iron fence enclosing the garden on the north side, some distance from the house, which Sir Hudson Lowe had installed to prevent cattle grazing in the vicinity from ravaging the flower beds. The governor had removed the ugly wooden fence previously erected for this purpose and replaced it with some extremely expensive cast-iron railings whose spikes were adorned at regular intervals with ornamental vases. Napoleon described these decorative railings as 'prison bars' and yet another 'cruel irony' inflicted on him by 'perfidious Albion'. What was truly ironic, however, was that the three massive slabs of stone covering his grave were taken from the kitchen of Longwood New House.

Contemporary watercolours and photographs of later date make it clear that Longwood New House, most of whose original fabric survived until its demolition just after the Second World War, must have been the finest property on St Helena apart from the governor's residence. Abbé Félix Coquereau, who assisted in the removal of Napoleon's remains in 1840, described it as 'a very handsome house with a slate roof and large windows'. Ernest d'Hauterive, who spent some time on St Helena in the early 1930s and made pilgrimages to the holy shrines of the Napoleon cult, summarized his impressions of Longwood New House as follows: 'The Emperor would surely have dwelt here under far better conditions. In these light, spacious, lofty rooms he would have had air and space in which to stroll about without being cramped by his retinue, as he was in his residence.'

Today, the highland plateau of Longwood presents a thoroughly deceptive appearance to the beholder, and so do the rooms in which Napoleon lived and died. These possess no more authenticity than a carefully arranged stage set. Nothing is as it really used to be; all is designed to accord as much as possible with the visitor's presentiments and foreknowledge. Longwood House is now, in its remoteness and heroic absurdity, a positively touching monument to French historical propaganda. In the case of The Briars, it is the weed-infested cable drums, the Cable & Wireless radio mast and the dilapidated Exiles Club with which 'perfidious Albion' intrudes upon the pilgrim's reverence. Here, one has to pass some wretched shacks and a shop with a petrol pump before gaining access to the well-kept grounds in which Longwood House is set. The picture its perfect condition presents would grace the window of any estate agent, especially as Longwood itself, which extends beyond the Longwood House estate, has since become the second largest township on St Helena.

On the other hand, Longwood as constituted today is far from presenting the appearance it did in Napoleon's time. That applies only to the front of the house, and thus to that part of the building in which the rooms used by Napoleon are situated. Only these were restored by Captain Masselin, the engineer officer who supervised renovation and reconstruction work from March 1859 onwards, whereas the largely timber-built annexes commissioned by Admiral Cockburn to house Napoleon's aides and servants were demolished at the same time. In other words, what now appears to be the whole of the original complex is really only half of it. This readily creates an entirely false impression of the actual size of the original property, which had to accommodate a household of as many as twenty-eight persons.

This very slapdash partial reconstruction was carried out thirty-eight years after Napoleon's death. That it happened at all may justifiably be regarded almost as a miracle made possible by the Napoleon cult which not only flourished during the Second Empire but received strong official backing. The ex-Emperor had scarcely breathed his last and been buried when the members of his household, already reduced by wastage, left the island he had hated with understandable alacrity. Longwood's library and furnishings, which had attained substantial proportions in the course of time, were auctioned off at Jamestown, and the house stood empty for two years. The then governor, Brigadier-General Walker, reported in June

1823 that 'the stables' – presumably he meant the timber annexes built by Admiral Cockburn – were in a ruinous state, and that their repair would cost a substantial sum. As for the old residence itself, notably the rooms used by Napoleon, these were suited at best to housing 'farm offices', especially as they did not lend themselves to conversion for a more useful or necessary purpose.

Thanks to the use which Governor Walker envisaged, the French officers who visited St Helena in 1840 in order to convey Napoleon's mortal remains to Paris were confronted on visiting Longwood by a truly horrific sight. The partition walls separating Napoleon's study and bedroom from the bathroom and valet's room beyond them had been demolished and the resulting area used as a cowshed, and a threshing machine had been installed in Napoleon's former drawing room and death chamber. Abutting on the outer walls of this room were a cowshed, pigsty and henhouse. In 1854, when Napoleon III entered into negotiations with the British Crown with a view to acquiring Longwood, the house and its land had two years earlier been leased to one Isaac Moss for a period of twenty-one years. Mr Moss had a very good head for business, because visitors desirous of watching the threshing machine at work in Napoleon's death chamber or casting a glance at the cows in his former study and bedroom had to pay one shilling for the privilege. For the house and the land immediately surrounding it, which represented only a fraction of the entire property, Moss demanded and received the exorbitant sum of £3,500. A contract excluding them from the lease was notarized on 20 July 1857.

Another thing that badly detracts from the look of the building as it used to be is the disappearance of the ring of tall, shady trees mentioned in her memoirs by Comtesse de Montholon and by a visitor to Longwood in September 1816, which enclosed the garden that was then laid out around the house. The same applies to the dense, ornamental islands of shrubs. These descriptions are confirmed by Marchand's well-known watercolour of 1819, which shows a spacious, elongated residence set in the midst of gardens, shrubs and trees. All this differs considerably from the stark architectural torso Longwood presents today, which resembles a prefabricated house temporarily erected on a bare studio stage as first prize in a television game show.

It may readily be imagined that, to Napoleon enthusiasts on pilgrimage to the scene of his martyrdom, Longwood House is the irrefutable, tangible proof of all that has been written about their hero's sufferings, hardships and deprivations in the Napoleonic 'gospels' and other 'holy scriptures'. Sadly, I was not lucky enough to meet any such pilgrim during my visit to this monument in July 2000. Furthermore, the custodian of the Napoleonic sites, France's honorary consul Michel Martineau – who inherited the post from his father Gilbert, incidentally – was away on leave. All I had in the way of a substitute, therefore, was the aforementioned guide book by the devout pilgrim Jean-Paul Kauffmann, whose big commercial success when published three years earlier provided me with a sufficient guarantee that the author's account of his impressions of St Helena and the feelings they aroused in him was thoroughly orthodox. And so, with a faint heart and Kauffmann as my cicerone, I climbed the stone steps leading up from the garden to the small terrace by way of which visitors enter Longwood House. Kauffmann has scarcely opened the veranda door and set foot in the entrance hall when he summarizes his first, spontaneous impression as follows: 'What promptly overwhelmed me was not the billiard table – it takes up almost the entire room – but the smell.' There follows a paragraph in which he expertly dissects the individual constituents of this smell, thereby revealing that his journalistic speciality is the assessment of wines.

This passage is both trivial and enlightening. The billiard table, which looks massive like all such pieces of furniture, measures 11ft 4ins by 6ft 1in, and the dimensions of the room in which it stands are 26ft 6ins by 17ft 6ins, the ceiling height being a lofty 12ft 4ins. Quite how, in view of these manifest differences in size, one can state that the billiard table occupies almost the entire room is a mystery that cannot be satisfactorily explained, even by pleading poetic licence. It does, in fact, strike a keynote that falsifies all the author's further impressions and harmonizes them with the mighty chorus of traditional complaints and grievances. Kauffmann's original contribution to the mantra of the Napoleonic Passion is his obsession with smell. Given the ex-Emperor's well-documented olfactory hypersensitivity, which was particularly evident at Longwood House, this is naturally a subject Kauffmann can exploit to even better advantage because, being a wine critic, he brings all the technical and terminological prerequisites to an idea no one had before him.

Enough said. Kauffmann's diary of his pilgrimage to St Helena provides a neat illustration of what happens when *déformation professionelle* is wedded to the fervour of a devotee. That union gives birth to the kind of hyperbole which speaks of 'the odour of tedium' or 'the incense of melancholy, the musk of the dark thoughts that impregnate the interior of the house'. It is hard to escape from the vaulting imagery bred by empathy as excessive as this. The smell that enveloped me in the entrance hall of Longwood House, which I endeavoured, after reading such a book, to identify with suspenseful attention, made my task easy: what came wafting towards me was the stuffy smell of an old, locked and long-empty wardrobe which one surreptitiously opens in the expectation of finding, if not a skeleton, at least a mysterious packet of letters enclosed by a lady's garter.

It was probably a long time since any visitor had entered the hall by way of the door to the terrace, so the room had been engulfed in airless gloom for days and weeks, possibly even months. No spacious Egyptian burial chamber, this, just another room in a seldom visited provincial museum. Like their predecessors as custodians of the *site mémorial de Longwood House*, the Martineaux, *père et fils*, have been extremely clever at nosing out and collecting household articles, both on the island and throughout the world, and reinstalling them where they were in Napoleon's day. Many of them had been utilized in Plantation House, the governor's residence, for instance the billiard table, a bookcase and some chairs. Other pieces of furniture had for generations been in the possession of families resident on St Helena, who parted with them, doubtless for a good price. Reproductions of the wallpaper, carpets and curtains, of which only a few scraps had survived, were manufactured in France. The termite-infested floorboards, window frames and beams were also faithfully reproduced.

But other items whose 'semi-certified' authenticity pilgrims set store by, especially here, turn out to be merely contemptible replicas. That applies particularly to the two folding iron camp beds with the green silk curtains, which were Napoleon's favourite aids to sleep and repose. Both of them, the bed on which he died in the drawing room of Longwood House and the one from his bedroom, are now in the Musée de l'Armée in Paris. Their original positions are now occupied by two structurally similar models, probably contemporary copies, for these light, practical and allegedly comfortable beds enjoyed great popularity even in Napoleon's lifetime, as witness a Parisian newspaper advertisement of August 1811: 'Iron beds. Patented invention. May be folded up like umbrellas. Most convenient, not only for travelling but also for setting up at home. Their elastic springs render mattresses unnecessary and thus facilitate the avoidance of insects. Obtainable from Desarches, metalworker, purveyor to His Majesty the King Emperor, 18, rue de Verneuil.'

In addition to the billiard table, the entrance hall contains two large globes. One celestial and the other terrestrial, they are the patently indispensable but superfluous stage props with which the mighty of every era have satisfied their urge to play. Charlie Chaplin demonstrated this by means of his wonderful slapstick ballet in *The Great Dictator*. (I myself possess a small, oval oil painting on cigar-box wood – the only 'political Spitzweg' in existence, as I jokingly call it. Napoleon, in the green uniform of the Imperial Guard, is depicted with a clay pipe in his mouth, blowing a big soap bubble on whose surface the outlines of the continents are faintly visible. Meanwhile, his little son the King of Rome, also bemedalled and in uniform, is chasing after it with childish enthusiasm.) After Napoleon's death, both globes were transferred to the Castle, the governor's official seat in Jamestown. On the basis of the memoirs of one of his servants, 'Mamelouck Ali', a selection of which was published in the 1920s, and in which these globes are mentioned, Octave Aubry, a distinguished Napoleonic scholar who spent some time on St Helena in 1932, was definitely able to identify them as belonging to the Napoleonic inventory of Longwood House.

I have never been particularly interested in old terrestrial globes because they necessarily reproduce the shape of the earth in a compressed form and in spherical projection, with the result that they convey a geographical certitude which they inevitably lack. Only ancient maps arouse one's irresistible curiosity with their blank, uncharted spaces, meandering, abbreviated coastlines, and rivers that peter out into nothingness. That was the only reason why I neglected to see whether St Helena was marked on Napoleon's globe.

At least where the rooms once used by Napoleon are concerned, Longwood House is, so to speak, an 'antimuseum'. In other words, those responsible have limited themselves to restoring the rooms more or less to their original condition and, for that reason, have deliberately avoided 'enriching' their bare, bleak appearance with a variety of knick-knacks such as tobacco jars, orders and medals, epaulettes or ceremonial swords. Objects of that kind can be found in the former library, whose original stock of several thousand volumes was impossible to reconstitute. Such is the desire for authenticity that characterizes the presentation of Napoleon's former living quarters that holes have been cut in the ever-drawn curtains over the windows facing the garden. The ex-Emperor, who did not want to be seen from outside, used to peer through these with his telescope. This practice seems all the more childish in that it turned the old saying on its head: the cat could look at the king, but the latter couldn't see the former.

If the rooms at Longwood resemble rooms in a doll's house, it is not because they were exceptionally small or cluttered with furniture, but because they represent a way of life, an attitude, which can no longer be reconstructed. What intensifies the oppressive feeling that assails one there into the sort of claustrophobia one sometimes experiences in a airless lift is the notion that one is treading the shadowy stage of a puppet theatre in which, when darkness falls, life-size marionettes perform a clumsy dance of the vampires. It fills one with horror to reflect that life 'at court', rigorously governed by etiquette, was confined mainly to the entrance hall, drawing room and dining room, and that it was carried on by Montholon and Bertrand and their wives, Las Cases, Gourgaud and Napoleon himself, in other words, by at least seven adults plus any visitors, children and domestic staff. The ladies *en grande toilette*, the gentlemen in full dress uniform, and all of them standing except during their brief meals or when expressly invited by Napoleon to sit down; interminable conversations about the same old topics or readings from the same old plays, preferably by Racine, whose alexandrines tend to become wearisomely monotonous when recited aloud – one cannot fail to be appalled by this vision of all the tedious rituals with which, until merciful fatigue brought them to a temporary close, elaborate but vain attempts were made to combat the expatriates' gnawing sense of futility – indeed, of the meaninglessness of their own existence – in this bizarre outpost of civilization.

One is filled not only with horror but with pity. Yes, pity for people who habitually mistook the world for a stage and their lives for roles. That applied as much to Napoleon as it did to his supporting cast of blockheads and nincompoops endowed with peasant cunning – shrewd penny-pinchers, each of whom calculated that his time of tribulation in exile would pay handsome dividends and felt assured of a brilliant future thereafter. Until then, the thing was to maintain one's composure – an impulse that soon waned, however. The household quickly became a snake-pit whose mutually suspicious occupants pursued one another with contempt and jealousy. Vanity proliferated, and every ego defended its rampant pretensions armed to the teeth. To quote Pascal's *Pensées*: "'This dog belongs to me,' said the poor children. 'That is my place in the sun.'" The behaviour of the household at Longwood is illustrative of this sceptical maxim.

Pilgrims and Napoleon enthusiasts will see much of this in the same light but perceive it quite differently, being committed to the example set by their idol. Like any theology, 'Napoleonology' is a form of study that aims at acquiring knowledge, but it suffers from one crucial limitation: it fails to explore its subject with due critical rigour. The living conditions to which Longwood House eloquently testifies, even today, are seen exclusively in the light of detailed descriptions left behind by persons immediately involved. Without exception, these are extremely partisan accounts which glorify as stoicism and heroism what could also be construed as an elaborate attempt to lend meaning to the meaningless. But even that endeavour is human – human in a somehow French fashion!

4

Napoleon's Last Battle

It is a curious fact that Napoleon always came to grief on islands. At the end of May 1793 he had to flee to France from his native Corsica, where he had been trying to satisfy his precocious ambitions, to escape the vengeance of the separatists who had always been rife there. The consequences of that setback were momentous, however, because it made a Frenchman of him.

He never even ventured to invade England, an undertaking for which he made elaborate preparations from June 1803 onwards, but he effortlessly masked the ignominious abandonment of that over-audacious plan by winning his most brilliant victory of all at Austerlitz on 2 December 1805.

This gained him mastery of the Continent, for one unspoken lesson he learned from the failure of his plan to invade England was that he never attempted to cross the Strait of Messina and drive the Bourbons, who were under British protection, out of Sicily. But another island almost sealed his fate at the zenith of his continental supremacy. After the militarily indecisive battle of Aspern on 21 and 22 May 1809, which was tantamount to a defeat because it damaged the myth of his invincibility, Napoleon and the bulk of his army were bogged down on the Danubian island of Lobau. What saved him from certain disaster was Archduke Charles's failure to follow up the Austrian forces' success the next day. Napoleon's penultimate stop on the road to his final downfall was Elba, which the victorious

Allied powers, with imprudent magnanimity, had assigned him as a sovereign state after his first abdication in 1814. He mistook that little island for a springboard that would catapult him back into power – an error he refused to acknowledge to his dying day.

Therein lies one of the most important reasons for the drama that unfolded on St Helena: on that remote rocky island, Napoleon was determined to remain true, not only to himself but also to the role he had played so successfully for so long. It was his last remaining trump card – one that no one would be able to contest, even given the circumstances of his exile. As he said to Las Cases: 'It is true that my fate is the exact opposite of other men's; their downfall usually diminishes them, where as mine has borne me upwards to an infinite extent. Each day delivers me from my semblance of being a tyrant, a murderer, a savage.'

St Helena as a purifying purgatory – that was theme on which Napoleon wanted to base the stage-management of his exile. That was why he had at all costs to avoid conceding that he had foundered on the sheer immoderation of his own pursuit of power. That, too, was why he insisted with seemingly childish obstinacy on being treated as an Emperor, even though the Allies had this time expressly stripped him of his rank and title. In his view, it was only logical to try to safeguard his son's claims to succession, just as he still continued to cling to the hope of transforming his destiny and refused to be a prisoner of the Allies. He also pledged his entourage to both these core elements in his strategy, thereby rendering them captives of his own folly.

For a long time, in fact, he was all the more successful in this because of his ability to impose the pace of events on his enemies. This was largely because he managed, even from a tiny speck thousands of miles away in the southern hemisphere, to project his shadow on Europe and present a constant threat there. By so doing he endeavoured to thwart the emergence of a new European order at odds with his own ideas. That was his old game, the one he could not bring himself give up even now, at the cost of self-surrender. The infinitely more difficult conditions under which he had to operate not only enhanced its appeal but held out the promise of an immense profit in return for a minimal investment. Such was the insane hope to which he clung, and which imbued him with the courage to prevail in circumstances that would have crushed a weaker man.

He was relying on his belief that the era of revolutionary upheaval he had represented would be followed in Europe by a widespread reaction that swept away all his emancipatory and progressive measures. This, he estimated, would lend his memory a new and seductive glamour. His aim being to accelerate and influence that process, he had to make every effort to impress his existence on the consciousness of the European public despite his banishment to an island lost in the wastes of the South Atlantic. And the most promising – indeed, the only – means of doing that was to persist in complaining of the conditions to which the victors were subjecting him in exile. Far from being designed primarily to secure him greater comfort and freedom of movement, his complaints were mainly propagandistic. Their object was to destroy the legitimacy of his tormentors, as he characterized those who had defeated him, and thus to undermine the basis of his exile.

But how to achieve this? The decision to banish Napoleon to St Helena had been taken principally because the island possessed all the prerequisites that would enable 'Europe's prisoner' to enjoy the greatest possible personal freedom. It was thought that this would take the wind out of the sails of anyone who complained that Napoleon was being treated with undue cruelty. At the same time, St Helena seemed to guarantee, not only that any attempt to escape would be futile, but also that the prisoner would be isolated, in other words, deprived from the first of any opportunity to influence public opinion in Europe. To the British government, which had been entrusted with the task of guarding him, both those considerations seemed to offer the greatest possible measure of security. They were, in fact, the very weaknesses which Napoleon exploited so relentlessly and with such skill.

He recognized, first, that the 'isolator' – the remote volcanic island on which the Allies intended to consign him to oblivion for the rest of his days – lent itself to use as a gigantic echo chamber. Every word uttered there, be it only in a whisper, was as audible in Europe as a peal of thunder. This alone guaranteed that his jailers' pedantry would rapidly degenerate into paranoia. His rocky prison was absolutely inaccessible, yet they went to the lengths of garrisoning it with nearly 3,000 soldiers and reinforcing them with over 500 cannon. As if that were not enough, Great Britain annexed and garrisoned Ascension, a barren and uninhabited island 700 miles north-west of St Helena, and the equally uninhabited island of Tristan da Cunha 1,300 miles to the south. This was in order to prevent either place from being used as a base for an attempt to free Napoleon. (Curiously enough, Ascension was administered until 1922 not as a 'territory' but as a 'stone frigate' under the supervision of the British Board of Admiralty. One result of this was that any children who first saw the light there were registered as having been born in Wapping.) Furthermore, three frigates and two smaller armed vessels maintained a constant state of readiness in the roads off Jamestown, and six more warships circled the island day and night.

But the interior of the island was also closely guarded. Lookouts were posted on all the major eminences, all the roads were watched, and anyone using them without a pass after nine o'clock at night was arrested. More troops were stationed at all strategically important points on the island, notably Jamestown itself and the three other places suitable for a landing: Rupert's Valley and Lemon Valley in the north, Sandy Bay in the south. Five hundred soldiers were housed in a tented encampment on the Deadwood plateau alone, where they could be seen from Longwood House, and the latter was enclosed by a low stone wall approximately four miles in circumference. At nightfall, the sentries posted along it within sight of each other took up their positions immediately around the house and remained there until daybreak.

Napoleon and his retinue were not, however, restricted in their movements by this security cordon. They were free to move throughout the Longwood and Deadwood plateau, which is some twelve miles in extent. If they wished to go beyond it they could do so, but only if accompanied by a British officer. A similar regulation applied to visits to Jamestown.

These and other security measures, which Napoleon and his staff regarded as needless humiliations, like the strict postal censorship to which they were subject, soon achieved the opposite of their intention. Thanks to their patently excessive nature, and to the extremely hidebound interpretation of all the very complicated and ever-changing regulations designed to keep Napoleon under constant surveillance – they were tightened up and relaxed by turns – his jailers and their political masters soon became thoroughly discredited.

Napoleon recognized that the strength his enemies sought to demonstrate was really a sign of weakness, because he could not fail to identify these security measures as unmistakable evidence of their abiding fear of him. But that, he inferred, was nothing more nor less than the negative expression of the power he still possessed and had to exploit. Such was the delusion he cherished and clung to. By so doing, he made life on St Helena hell for himself and his motley staff, whose members had voluntarily accompanied him into exile from a mixture of motives including genuine admiration and affection, but also in the sure expectation of profiting from the experience. Responsibility for this could readily be attributed to the perfidy of their custodians, who brilliantly fulfilled their scapegoat's role thanks to the manifest paranoia of the head jailer, Sir Hudson Lowe, who reached St Helena on 14 April 1816. By the time he appeared on the scene, Napoleon and his company of amateur players had successfully completed their rehearsals for his illusory show of strength. From now on, everything went like clockwork.

Napoleon's theatrical production, which lent his propaganda its indispensable substratum of credibility, was staged with such skill that it is misconstrued, even today, as a genuine drama – as the 'Passion' of a 'secular Saviour'. This conception of it is based upon the reading and emphatic interpretation of the 'St Helena gospels'. Their devotees fail to recognize, however, that the evidentiary status ascribed to those 'gospels' refers only to what happened on-stage. In other words, they misconstrue theatrical reality as fact and regard the cast, not as actors, but as victims of fate.

That illusion is attested largely by the very thing capable of damaging it: the dramatis personae sometimes slipped out of character, gave vent to their mutual dislike, displayed jealousy and anger, and loudly complained of their all too understandable 'islanditis'. Although Napoleon sometimes encouraged the tensions this created, court intrigues being a welcome source of amusement to him, even in exile, he could not allow this play within a play to impair the effect of the actual production, and he took the greatest care that no word of it reached the outside world. However, the more often the hopes he pinned on this production were dashed – he expected it to bring about a major change on the European political stage and was deluded enough to believe that he would be summoned back to direct it in the capacity of a saviour – the more uncertain his fellow actors became about the point of their activities, and, above all, about their duration.

Two members of the cast who threatened to crack under the strain escaped by simply abandoning their roles and quitting the Longwood House stage in a hurry. The first was Las Cases, who made at least some attempt to camouflage his abrupt exit, albeit in a very obvious manner. Every member of the court except Napoleon himself was free to leave the island subject to the governor's permission. However, Las Cases could not bring himself to take this step because he had long planned to publish his conversations with Napoleon from the beginning of his exile onwards, and such overt disloyalty on his part would have compromised him badly. With an eye to the future success of his publishing project, therefore, he had the bright idea of provoking his own dismissal. With this in mind he resorted to an extremely clumsy but, in view of Sir Hudson Lowe's paranoia, thoroughly effective trick. In January 1817 he entrusted two long missives to a mulatto named James Scott, who had occasionally run secret errands for him in the past but had not escaped the ever-vigilant governor's attention. Scott, who was about to accompany his master to Europe, was instructed to take the letters with him and deliver them there.

Scott's mission came to light, the letters sewn into the lining of his jacket were discovered, and Las Cases was arrested. He had blatantly violated a regulation, twice endorsed by himself, according to which no letters could be dispatched without the governor's prior knowledge.

The whole point of Las Cases's smuggling venture was that it should fail, for the inmates of Longwood House had other, more secure ways of corresponding with Europe unbeknown to Sir Hudson Lowe. So the sole purpose of his 'reckless' act was to bring about his summary expulsion. He had already collected enough material for his planned work on Napoleon and knew that his source had been very largely tapped, nor could he afford to miss the opportune moment for the publication of his book. After all, who could guarantee that Napoleon, if he survived for long enough, would not outlive Las Cases himself? All his efforts and privations would then have been in vain.

Las Cases acted in accordance with the logic of his ambition. That accounts for his calm demeanour when arrested. It also explains why he rejected all the compromises Sir Hudson Lowe suggested, even though their acceptance would have enabled him to remain on St Helena in Napoleon's company. A third indication that Las Cases was seeking to enforce his departure is that he declined a final interview with Napoleon and the chance to speak with anyone else on his staff. He was obviously afraid of having to justify his foolish conduct and, thus, of revealing his true motives. That would have detracted from the success of his projected publication. Who would have believed a traitor, a second Judas who had betrayed his master and deserted him for the sake of literary ambition? If he could maintain the fiction of his expulsion, on the other hand, it could only be to the advantage of himself and his book's success. The British government and Sir Hudson Lowe, in particular, would then be exposed to a charge of inhumane perfidy: Las Cases, the truest of the true, the 'favourite disciple', had been brutally and arbitrarily wrested away from his master simply for daring, in a spirit of self-sacrificial loyalty, to publicize his sufferings in Europe through the medium of two letters. This episode shows how well La Cases had grasped the purpose of Napoleon's *mise en scène*, which aimed to put 'perfidious Albion' in the wrong and subject it to an incessant barrage of accusations before the court of European public opinion.

The other quitter possessed neither the cunning nor the intelligence of a man like Las Cases, hence the brutal candour with which he explained his motives for leaving to all who cared to listen. The thoroughgoing 'islanditis' from which General Gourgaud was suffering came to a head at Christmas 1816, when he challenged Count Montholon, his companion in misfortune, to a duel over some foolish triviality. Napoleon had to step in because nothing could have been more detrimental to his strategy *vis-à-vis* the governor than a public altercation between members of his immediate circle. On 25 December 1816, he read his squabbling lieutenants the riot act. They led a comfortable life, he told them – indeed, a happy one. They could go riding whenever and wherever they chose, accompanied only by a British officer, and were excellently provided for. If they complained, it was only because they had to. Moreover, they were free to leave the island at any time. They could rely on a warm reception wherever they went, having enough to talk about to last them the rest of their days, and any great power would be delighted to employ them in posts befitting their rank. They would be graciously received by the Emperors of Russia and Austria – even by the Bourbons in France. This betrayed the illusions that nourished Napoleon's vain belief that he would get another chance to triumph over his adversaries.

But his remarks to Gourgaud are most revealing of himself: 'What does it matter to me that you're a man of honour? You should devote yourself solely to the task of pleasing me. You have wild, untamed characteristics [...]. I suppose you imagined, when you came here, that you were my comrade, but I'm no one's comrade. Nor can anyone give me orders. You would like to be the focal point here, like the sun among the planets, but that position befits me alone. You're the cause of all the vexations that have plagued me since we've been here. [...] If you're really so bad a fellow that you cannot stop picking quarrels with Montholon, it would certainly be better for you to leave us.'

Gourgaud, a hypersensitive man consumed with boredom, must have been profoundly hurt by these unvarnished words. It was the general's very sensitivity that used to irritate Napoleon and prompt him to say harsh things he sometimes regretted. He would then try to restore Gourgaud's wounded pride by showering him with conciliatory gestures and tokens of affection. But all these attentions were futile because Napoleon himself did not mean them seriously. One even gains the impression that he derived a kind of sadistic pleasure from the bullying for which Gourgaud made an ideal victim and with which he sought to dispel the boredom that afflicted him too. Only this can explain why Napoleon one day told Gourgaud that he had been born among the *canaille* and would always remain *canaille* – a calculated and insulting allusion to the general's humble origins (he came from a family of actors). He added that Gourgaud owed his rapid social advancement solely to him, the Emperor.

Gourgaud, who was extremely proud of his courage and efficiency, could not have been more cruelly offended. Little less hurtful, however, were Napoleon's repeated predictions that Gourgaud would go insane, or his remarks to other people – who would, he could be sure, pass them on to the man himself – to the effect that Gourgaud would commit suicide. When these bore no fruit, Napoleon formally instructed Bertrand to advise the general to end his own life. He eventually went so far as to tell Gourgaud to his face that one pistol shot could put him out of his misery at any time.

The alternate bullying and flattery to which Gourgaud was exposed, in addition to the boredom that never ceased to plague him, continued for a year or more. On 2 February 1818 he informed Napoleon that, in view of Montholon's persistent insults, he had decided to challenge him to a duel for the second time. Napoleon responded by flying into a rage. He called Gourgaud a bandit and a murderer, said he would have to duel with himself, Napoleon, instead of Montholon, and – in true Corsican fashion – threatened to put a curse on him.

This was Napoleon's way of conveying, quite unmistakably, that he had grasped that he himself was the real object of Gourgaud's hatred, which was fuelled mainly by unrequited love. Napoleon had not only disappointed him; he had clearly intimated his unwillingness to reciprocate the affection Gourgaud thought he could expect in return for his self-sacrifice in voluntarily sharing his master's exile. Gourgaud plunged ever deeper into a maelstrom of despair, hence his response to Napoleon's cynical advice to put a bullet in his head: he proposed that all the members of the household should shut themselves up in a room, drink plenty of champagne, and be slowly suffocated by the poisonous fumes of a coal fire. To Gourgaud this already seemed the only conceivable way out of his desperate predicament, but it also showed that, unlike Las Cases, he had never fathomed Napoleon's strategy. His future conduct provided ample proof of this.

Gourgaud's second challenge to Montholon proved his deliverance. Napoleon informed the general via Bertrand that he wished him to request the governor for permission to depart, pleading ill health. He was also to address a similar letter to himself, the Emperor. Gourgaud refused, observing that Napoleon merely wished to create the impression that he, Gourgaud, was deserting him, whereas it was His Majesty who was driving him away. This final act of rebellion snapped Gourgaud's chains once and for all. On 7 January 1818 he called on Sir Hudson Lowe and requested permission to leave Longwood House: 'I have been treated like a dog. I would rather die in a French prison than continue to live here, playing the role of a courtier and thereby losing my last vestige of independence.'

But that was only the prelude to the torrent of words with which Gourgaud vented the hatred in his heart until he sailed for England four weeks later. He treated all who cared to listen to a candid account of life and conditions in Longwood House. Probably without realizing it, and simply because he hadn't grasped them himself, he disclosed important elements of Napoleon's strategy. Convinced that he would not have to end his days on St Helena, said Gourgaud, Napoleon persisted in believing that, once back in power, the liberal Whigs would promptly release him. Nor had he given up hope of reascending the throne of France. Did Napoleon have a chance of escaping from the island? He could have done so on at least ten occasions and still could, nothing being impossible for someone with millions at his disposal. Nevertheless, said Gourgaud, although the Emperor had given him much cause for complaint, he would not betray him. That was why he merely repeated that Napoleon could easily escape to America whenever he chose. If escape was so easy, he was asked, why didn't he resolve on that step? Everyone had urged him to do so, Gourgaud replied, but he had always disputed the arguments they advanced and declined every time. Even though he led a miserable existence here, he was secretly delighted by the close attention devoted to his exile; in particular, by the great interest accorded it by the European powers and the fact that even his most trivial complaints and utterances were always carefully noted. He had often observed: 'I can no longer live as a private person; I prefer to be a prisoner here than dwell as a free man in the United States.'

These statements are evidence of Gourgaud's hatred and stupidity. That Napoleon had had a chance to escape was a wholly unfounded assertion disproved not only by the genuinely all-embracing measures taken to foil any such attempt, but by the island's rugged terrain. Even to cross it would have required the skills of an experienced mountaineer, and those Napoleon truly didn't possess, even though he had once crossed the snowy St Gotthard – and occasionally slithered down it on the seat of his pants. Even if he had succeeded, however, he wouldn't have got further than Sandy Bay in the south of the island. Despite this, Sir Hudson Lowe listened eagerly to Gourgaud's effusions because they chimed only too well with his own fears. These attained such a pitch that they often robbed him of sleep, causing him to gallop to Longwood House in the middle of the night and submit the sentries posted there to intensified supervision.

Gourgaud's stupidity is attested, in particular, by his incomprehension of Napoleon's motives in failing to take advantage of these alleged opportunities to escape. He was not concerned about his personal freedom, as Gourgaud obtusely claimed. The last thing he wanted was an existence like that of his elder brother Joseph, who had safely made it to America, where he was now living as the wealthy Comte de Survilliers on his comfortable country estate at Bordentown, Connecticut. Napoleon had a very cogent reason for this: he went in constant fear for his life, believing that his enemies were out to assassinate him. That was why, on the one night he spent in Jamestown, he had a stout bolt fitted to his bedroom door in addition to the existing lock, so that it could be secured from within. This bolt continued for many years to be an object of interest to visitors retracing his steps on the island.

Far more important than fear, however, was a quite different motive: Napoleon's prime and abiding concern was power, not freedom. To him, that alone lent meaning to his life. Even in exile, which was intended to condemn him to impotence, his elixir of life was still to wield power, to put the fear of god into others, and – as even naive Gourgaud realized – to compel the monarchs of Europe to continue to give him their undivided attention. No, Gourgaud and others failed to understand Napoleon or discern his obsessive desire to be able to gamble successfully for the acquisition of power, which meant everything to him, even on far-off St Helena.

But the creative superiority with which Napoleon staged his production is apparent from two facts: not only did it escape detection by its principal players, notably Gourgaud, but it was undisrupted by the precipitate departure of two of their number. What saw to that was Napoleon's main opponent, who was perfectly cast in the dramatically indispensable role of model villain. Almost everyone who met Sir Hudson Lowe described him as an inordinately unlikable, narrow-minded, insecure and ultra-suspicious man who was utterly devoid of tact and diplomatic finesse. The imputation is that it was precisely those shortcomings which had prompted the British government to entrust him with such a tricky assignment, and that, since Napoleon's life had been spared rather than summarily cut short, there were no grounds for appointing a jailer who would make his detention as pleasant as possible. This conjecture is, however, coloured by the popular notion of 'perfidious Albion'. It may simply be that no gentleman would have been prepared to accept such an undignified post. What rendered it irresistible to Hudson Lowe was the knighthood that went with the job, the rank of lieutenant-general, a very handsome annual salary of £12,000, and the almost certain prospect of further honours and promotions if he carried out his mission satisfactorily.

It was easy to suspect Sir Hudson Lowe of such ambitions because all he had to show was a hitherto undistinguished and generally ill-starred military career. It is written of him that he had never held the sort of really responsible post that would have given him scope for decision-making and the freedom to issue orders of his own. Invariably dependent on the goodwill and orders of others, he had never learnt to act on his own initiative. Moreover, unconditional obedience had become second nature to him. These, however, were the worst possible qualifications for filling such an important post so far from his superiors. Enquiries, requests for official rulings and other information took over six months to get from St Helena to London and back again. This delay in resolving problems, most of them merely trivial, which a freer and more independent spirit would have dealt with at once, inevitably led to friction, conflicts and misunderstandings. And that, of course, was extremely welcome to Napoleon because it supplied him with a pretext for introducing new elements and ploys into his game.

An additional factor was that Napoleon owed his success very largely to an ability to command. This was bound to place Lowe in a thoroughly awkward position *vis-à-vis* his prisoner, especially as he always insisted on their formal parity of rank: in accordance with his instructions, Lieutenant-General Sir Hudson Lowe always addressed Napoleon as 'General Bonaparte', a designation always rejected by the latter, who insisted upon the title 'Emperor'. However, these purely protocollary trivia were indicative of a genuine difference in rank which could not fail to keep putting the jailer in the wrong as regards his prisoner. That alone was enough to provide the increasingly acrimonious conflict between the two men with a continuous supply of ammunition.

Their ongoing dispute, which Napoleon sometimes garnished with the most spiteful personal insults – insults which show that not even he was immune to slipping out of character – is always regarded as the main drama that unfolded on St Helena. Seen in that light, Napoleon emerges as the far superior moral victor, for his death signalled a kink in Sir Hudson Lowe's career. After a brief stint as deputy governor of Ceylon, he ended his life in obscurity, abused, disgraced and impoverished. His crucial mistake was to fulfil his jailer's role in strict conformity with his superiors' wishes, with a meticulousness that verged on parody. They distanced themselves from him as soon as his work was done, rewarding him with ingratitude and punishing him with contempt. The final verdict on him was passed by the Duke of Wellington in the course of a conversation with Earl Stanhope in October 1837: 'Without being any great admirer of Sir Hudson Lowe, I must say that I think he has been shamefully used about this business – shamefully.'

In fact, Napoleon looked upon his battles with Sir Hudson Lowe, militarily speaking, as a mere diversion. He always made it clear that Lowe was not a worthy opponent, just a welcome minion to be thrashed at will, a means of attracting royal and public attention back in Europe. Napoleon did not argue with Lowe in order to obtain better living conditions for himself and his staff in their involuntary exile; he used him simply as a whipping-boy. The altercations about forms of address, censorship, diet, medical treatment and restricted freedom of movement – the ever-recurring complaints about wind and weather and the structural defects of Longwood House, the eternal clamour which filled page after page of the 'evangelists'' accounts and, if only for that reason, attracted widespread attention – were merely pretexts designed to produce one thing alone: an incessant din.

The Duke of Wellington, in his coolly pragmatic way, discerned this later on. His conversation with Earl Stanhope embodied the following comments on the subject: 'If, however, I had been Lord Bathurst, I would have adopted a different plan for his confinement. There are only very few landing-places along the coast of St Helena. These I would have strictly guarded, and insisted upon his showing himself to an English officer every night and morning, and then for the rest of the time I would have let him do or go wherever he pleased. This would have avoided most matters of dispute, and then he might have received or sent as many letters as he chose.'

But common sense of that kind was not in the nature of Lord Bathurst, still less of a man like Sir Hudson Lowe, which was why they played into

Napoleon's hands. Nothing could have been more welcome to him than pretexts for everlasting complaints. They alone ensured that the attention devoted to his fate in Europe did not diminish. He wanted it to pave the way for the triumphal return he was long deluded enough to consider possible. That alone was the focus of all his sometimes febrile expectations.

It had become clear that Napoleon had lost all his political nous and succumbed to megalomania back in the summer of 1813, even before the so-called 'Battle of the Nations' at Leipzig. What supplied the final proof that he had lost all sense of reality was his inflexible attitude in the winter of 1814, when he was up to his neck in water and the Allies disconcerted him by advancing on France after all. Even at that stage, he spurned all opportunities for a compromise peace that would have salvaged his throne because, to the very last, he nursed the vain hope that a great military victory would turn the tide in his favour. Nothing ever cured him of that delusion, not even the second abdication enforced on him by the victorious powers.

During his weeks-long voyage to St Helena, Napoleon developed this loss of reality into the insane system to which he harnessed his entourage, whose members were no more able to discern the sheer lunacy of his *mise en scène* than he was to deal with the paranoid way in which Sir Hudson Lowe reacted to it. This is apparent from the message of the 'gospels', but they also reveal how firmly imprisoned Napoleon was in his own delusions. Illustrative of this are their descriptions of life 'at court', where he imposed the strictest observance of etiquette on his household. That this sycophantic ballet company should have gone through its paces in the thoroughly unsuitable confines of Longwood House, where matters were additionally complicated by the presence of a needlessly numerous domestic staff, is a thought that defies the imagination.

Napoleon insisted on this grandiose fiction not simply because it was a comforting reminder of the past, but because he saw it as something which, after his involuntary interlude on St Helena, would become a reality once more. The same confident belief is also betrayed by many of the remarks he made during his first three years of exile, when he still clung to the hope that a fundamental shift of opinion, whatever occasioned it, would prompt the British to bring him back to Europe, if not release him altogether. His expectations were founded on an unrealistic interpretation of the news and rumours that reached St Helena by way of newspapers or ships' crews. Thanks to them, he had some idea of developments in Europe and knew of the many reactionary measures taken by the Bourbons to underpin their regime, which was shaky from the start.

Napoleon followed events in England with the same attention, but his total failure to understand them only made the speculations he based on them all the wilder. He expected much of a Whig return to power and hoped that the highly unpopular Prince Regent would be succeeded by Princess Charlotte, whom he knew to be very sympathetic towards him and his fate. In the same connection, he kept harping on the enthusiastic public welcome he had received when the *Bellerophon* dropped anchor off the English coast and countless jam-packed boats came hurrying out to pay their respects. Although it was natural of him to confuse simple curiosity with sympathy for himself and his cause, sober reflection should have taught him better.

The political webs he spun from all these threads had their counterpart in the numerous harebrained schemes that were being hatched in America with a view to abducting him from St Helena. Many veterans of the *Grande Armée* who saw no future for themselves in France had fled to the United States, sometimes with the overt encouragement of the Bourbons, who were only too happy to get rid of potential troublemakers. Members of Napoleon's 'Old Guard', in particular, formed the hard core of the 'Champ d'Asile' which came into being in the future state of Texas. The wide-open spaces of the Wild West and the seaports of North and South America were seething with Napoleonic emigrants skilled in nothing but the soldier's trade. Like Philippe Brideau, Balzac's protagonist in the third part of *Les Célibataires*, they were only waiting for Napoleon to return and offer them a chance to win fresh glory.

Individuals like Brideau nursed a lunatic ambition: the forming of a huge empire, organized by none other than Napoleon, out of the then-disintegrating Spanish colonies of South and Central America. The first step, therefore, would be to release him from exile. That was the origin of all the absurd abduction plans with which the French ambassador to Washington, Hyde de Neuville, alarmed the authorities in Paris as soon as he heard of them, and they, in their turn, had nothing better to do than to alert the victorious powers. Napoleon, who occasionally learned of these fanciful schemes, treated them with unadulterated scorn and derision. He himself was pursuing other figments of the imagination. Only his death preserved him from hearing of one final, bitter irony: he died just as his supporters in New Orleans finished building a two-storeyed house at the intersection of Chartres and St Louis Streets – the one in which they meant him to reside after making a successful escape.

Napoleon's wild dreams, of which he never despaired, sustained two hard knocks. The first was the arrival of the commissioners whom victorious Russia and Austria had sent to St Helena by prior arrangement, their task being to satisfy themselves of Napoleon's presence there. Prussia had dispensed with the commissioner to which it was entitled, probably for reasons of expense, whereas France insisted on sending a representative of its own. On hearing of the commissioners' arrival in mid-June 1816, Napoleon jumped to the erroneous conclusion that they had been sent to him by their sovereigns as envoys plenipotentiary. Not only did their arrival seem to confirm his claims to imperial rank, but he assumed that they had been officially instructed to hold exploratory discussions with him about the possibility of his return to power.

Sir Hudson Lowe dispelled this pipe-dream a few days later. In response to Napoleon's enquiries via Bertrand, he informed him that the commissioners had not come bearing any messages from their sovereigns. Only then did Napoleon grasp that the men sent him by the royal courts of Europe – by his friend Tsar Alexander I and his father-in-law the Emperor of Austria – were watchdogs, not envoys. No longer their 'brother', as those monarchs had formerly addressed him in their letters, he was just an ordinary prisoner.

The second blow that finally shattered Napoleon's illusions was the Congress of Aix-la-Chapelle convened by the Allied powers in November 1818.

Among other things, it approved a resolution drafted by Napoleon's old foe and fellow Corsican, Count Pozzo di Borgo, which aimed to reinforce the principle of his exile. Its wording aptly described Napoleon as 'the power of revolution concentrated in one individual', who was thus 'the prisoner of Europe'. As for his numerous complaints about the conditions of his exile, they were both 'false and childish', and intended only 'to excite the sympathy of his adherents'. The passing of this resolution on 21 November 1818, unanimously and without debate, put paid to Napoleon's illusions once and for all: from now on, there was no prospect of his leaving St Helena alive.

The resolutions passed at the Congress of Aix-la-Chapelle became known on St Helena at the beginning of March 1819. They plunged Napoleon into the deepest despair. For days he never showed his face, even to his immediate circle. His valet, Marchand, was the only person who saw him, but he couldn't coax a word out of him. Napoleon realized that the game was up at last. It was a case of *rien ne va plus*. On 2 April 1819 he received his last visitor, a cousin of Lord Liverpool, the British prime minister. That gentleman, Ricketts by name, later made a verbatim record of their conversation. It showed that Napoleon was a broken man, both physically and mentally. The *mise en scène* on which he had pinned so many hopes had failed; now, he merely begged that his lot be eased, and that he be delivered from the clutches of Sir Hudson Lowe, whose regime he characterized with his well-known litany of complaints. No longer hopeful of regaining power, he was simply concerned to end his days under more agreeable circumstances. But even that request, which he implored his last visitor to pass on, was not to be fulfilled. Whatever one's view of Napoleon, one cannot but describe this as tragic.

It is surely no coincidence that Napoleon's health deteriorated rapidly thereafter. The Congress of Aix-la-Chapelle had, in a sense, condemned him to death. From now on he began to be consumed by the cancer of which his father had died before him. To associate the final blighting of Napoleon's hopes with the onset of that disease is psychosomatically plausible. On 5 May 1821, death mercifully released him from the slough of despond in which he had since been living.

5

The Homecoming

No sooner had Napoleon died than his devotees transfigured him in a way that long prevented historians from undertaking a critical assessment of his life and achievements. St Helena, his place of exile, played a central role in this 'canonization' process. His alleged martyrdom on that remote rocky island, based on the testimony of his 'evangelists', became the principal evidence in favour of his sanctification, his apotheosis. In close conjunction with this, the circumstances of his imprisonment, the island's hostile environment, his deliberate maltreatment by tormentors who systematically denied him any relief and housed and fed him with extreme inadequacy – all these threads were woven into an ever vaster, ever more detailed tapestry illustrative of human vileness and cruelty. Although it dispensed with any first-hand inspection of the 'scene of the crime' and neglected to undertake an impartial, critical appraisal of the first-hand evidence for which the 'gospels' were mistaken, this version continues to colour the image of Napoleon presented by the numerous biographies devoted to the Emperor, which are addressed to a wide public. Their picture of him has long ago congealed into one of those living lies that help to constitute a nation's idea of its place in history.

Napoleon's apotheosis, which was decisively influenced by himself at the time of his exile, and which was intended to exert a directly propagandistic effect, now acquired a life of its own and gathered momentum. His exile and death promoted him to the status of a saint whose veneration consoled and fortified all those who had been disadvantaged by the advent of reactionary conditions in Europe. Foremost among them were members of the *Grande Armée* whose lives were inextricably bound up with his regime: the ex-soldiers and numerous officials in the military administration – in short, the Napoleonic civil service elites for whom the Bourbon government had no use because they were regarded as generally suspect. Through them, however, Napoleon rapidly developed into a national myth that proliferated in almost every European country except Spain and Russia. This seems all the more paradoxical when one reflects that those countries had lived under his yoke, and that adverse memories of his rule were still fresh in people's minds. The popularization of the St Helena 'gospels', particularly Las Cases's *Mémorial*, which was translated immediately after its publication in 1823, presented a new and seductive picture of a conqueror and despot whose sole aim had been to promote freedom and prosperity among the nations. Thanks to this new image, authenticated by his martyrdom in exile, Napoleon soon became the idol not only of the liberals, but of all who suffered from a sense of deprivation as a result of the reactionary political and social conditions that had come into being in Europe after his downfall.

This picture was propagated and popularized mainly by an abundance of non-political anecdotes and edifyingly entertaining narratives that emphasized his human qualities alone, likewise by hastily cobbled-together 'historical' novels which enjoyed a great vogue. Especially characteristic of the Napoleonic myth that became established so quickly, however, is a narrative strand that simply disavowed the hero's death on St Helena and made his successful escape the starting point for all manner of fanciful hypotheses. One example is Adolph von Schaden's novel *Jussuph Pascha* (1829), which spun the yarn that Napoleon had escaped from his rocky prison 'on the day of his supposed death' and, after making an adventurous getaway, reached the court of Constantinople, where he led the Ottoman Empire to renewed power and glory. This thoroughly entertaining novel was merely an elaboration of the assertions contained in a pamphlet published a year earlier. Its appealing title: 'Ten most important reasons for supposing that Hussein Pasha, commander-in-chief of the Ottoman armies, is Napoleon resurrected and returned.'

In contrast to the new and refulgent image of Napoleon with which his literary mythicization embarked on its career, the collective perception of the horrific scene of his 'Passion' invented a romantic St Helena which had little more in common with the real island than its name. That tiny fragment of the British Empire was thereby invested with incomparable importance. Thanks to the immense resonance of the Napoleonic legend, the far-off island became a focal point for acquired ideas claiming association with providence, with the great laws that form the origin of human progress, with the will and hand of God, the workings of the universe, or the meaning of history. St Helena thus became, as it were, the Archimedean point that determined the fate of Napoleon: the 'world soul', as Hegel once characterized him. Without reference to that fateful speck in the vastness of the ocean, that place where a dream was finally shattered but, at the same time, perpetuated into an everlasting challenge, ideas of the hero could not fully accord with his portrayal by the 'gospels'. That was how St Helena became the focal point at which the meaning of world history was concentrated, and from which it radiated outwards.

This overloading of the distant island with significance, a process which did not attain full intensity until after Napoleon's death, has exerted a lasting influence on people's ideas about the place. St Helena has been tinged with deepest melancholy by the abundance of pictures which show the lonely hero in silent communion with the waves forever breaking on the island's bizarre, rocky shores; which allegorize him as an eagle chained to a rugged cliff; which depict his solitary figure silhouetted against an infinite expanse lit by the setting sun; or which portray him as Prometheus. Compared to them, imaginary scenes of Hell and Purgatory make a positively cheerful impression. They, by contrast, tell of the beginning and end of the world. *Nec ultra*. Rooted in romanticism, the Napoleon cult transformed St Helena into a cipher, a 'death island' par excellence.

News of Napoleon's death reached Paris at the beginning of July 1821.

It relieved the Restoration not only of its fears but also of a heavy burden: there now seemed to be a chance of reconciling the 'two Frances', the one that had persisted in pinning its hopes on Napoleon and the one represented by the Bourbons. This deceptive peace was soon disrupted, however. As early as 7 July 1821, General Gourgaud wrote Grand Duchess Stephanie of Baden a letter in which he demanded that '[Napoleon's] corpse be wrested from the hands of his unworthy foes. Let us all unite in an endeavour to ensure that his mortal frame be conveyed to his family in Rome. It is there, in that soil trodden by so many heroes before him, that the great Napoleon must find his eternal repose.' On 15 August, Napoleon's mother addressed a similar request to Lord Castlereagh, the British foreign secretary, who did not deign to reply. Montholon and Bertrand, Napoleon's executors, were both staying in England after their return from St Helena. Not until 21 September, when they endorsed her plea in a missive to George IV, were they formally advised that Great Britain regarded itself simply as the custodian of 'General Bonaparte's' mortal remains, and that these would be handed over, either to France or to his family, as soon as the French government submitted a request to that effect.

On 19 July 1821, even before the British had clarified their position in regard to this politically sensitive matter, a petition had been lodged in the French Chamber. Although it remained unanswered, the message was clear: the Restoration regime had no wish to be troubled with the matter at any price. Silence also greeted a petition signed by Montholon, Bertrand and Marchand, which they addressed to Louis XVIII in person in the spring of 1822. This requested that the dead Emperor be interred beside his father at Ajaccio in Corsica.

The restored Bourbons' intransigence was initially emulated by Louis Philippe, the 'Citizen King', who was brought to power by the July Revolution of 1830. This was rather inconsistent, given that his regime sought to base its legitimacy on the claim to represent 'Toutes les Gloires de la France', as it said in big gold letters on the tympanum of the Palais de Versailles, which was extensively renovated without delay. It soon turned out that there were certain exceptions to this rule. These became all the more noticeable when Louis Philippe made every effort to use the primarily nostalgic and quite unpolitical Napoleon cult, which had been rampant for a long time, to secure his regime. Napoleon and the Empire occupied a particularly prominent place among the historical references that were so loudly invoked. Prime evidence of this is the fact that the July Monarchy swiftly completed the Arc de Triomphe, the classical edifice intended to glorify the victories of Napoleon's armies, which had not progressed beyond its foundations by 1815. Another noteworthy example was the return of Napoleon's statue to the top of the bronze column in the Place Vendôme. Against this, however, the previous regime's residence ban on members of the former Emperor's family was expressly re-emphasized in August 1832.

This seems all the more paradoxical when one considers that the 'Citizen Monarchy' entertained no animosity towards representatives of the old, Napoleonic administrative elite. On the contrary, the latter formed the very backbone of France's major state institutions. Louis Philippe had sworn his constitutional oath in the presence of a gathering dominated by marshals of the empire, and his principal consultative body, the Conseil d'État, was teeming with former ministers and dignitaries of the Napoleonic empire. What was more, Louis Philippe relied mainly on experienced Napoleonic generals to complete the conquest of Algeria, which the Restoration had begun. However, this seemingly singular practice accorded with a set of political circumstances that had developed in France since Napoleon's first abdication in 1814. That change of government had been consummated only by Napoleon's retirement, not by that of his senior officials, most of whom actually promoted the Bourbon restoration because it seemed to them to be in their own best interests. That was why Napoleon had accused them of treachery.

Although most of the Napoleonic dignitaries were squeezed out of their new posts as the Bourbons proceeded to consolidate their hold on power, they continued to prevail within the political system by simply sloughing off their Napoleonic skin and mutating into liberals. Balzac captured this surprising transformation in his novel *Le Député d'Arcis*:

'Bonapartists turned into liberals, for, thanks to one of the most curious metamorphoses, nearly all Napoleon's soldiers became transformed into ardent supporters of the constitutional system.' It was these same liberals who came to power with the July Revolution and, consequently, assumed another new name: from now on they styled themselves 'Orleanists', devout supporters of the constitutional monarchy represented by Louis Philippe d'Orléans.

Therein lies the key to this apparent paradox: they were 'Napoleonists', not 'Bonapartists'; that is to say, they were proud to acknowledge the man to whom they owed everything – titles, honours, material prosperity – but more than happy to know that he was in his Valhalla. Above all, they had no need to fear that he would snatch away the power they now held and were officially permitted to wield by Louis Philippe. In other words, the last thing they wanted was a resumption of the Napoleonic epic, whatever form it might take. That was history and must remain so. The same thing applied to the Emperor's mortal remains, which were safe on St Helena. It would be imprudent to relinquish them to his family, let alone convey them to Paris, because any such undertaking would be fraught with political symbolism and could easily give rise to friction and misunderstandings.

This explains why the July Monarchy began by firmly and repeatedly rejecting all endeavours to bring Napoleon's body home from his place of exile. No fundamental change in this attitude occurred until 1 March 1840, when the premiership passed to Adolphe Thiers, who had occasionally spoken out in favour of repatriation. A historian, Thiers had devoted fifteen years to writing a monumental history of the Revolution and the Napoleonic regime under contract to the publisher Paulin, who was guaranteeing him a lucrative advance of half a million francs. This was common knowledge, hence the logical supposition, put about by malicious tongues, that his support for the return of Napoleon's remains was just a gigantic publicity stunt designed to promote the sale of his multi-volume history.

No less plausible was the theory that the government intended this spectacular coup to divert public attention from its disastrous policy in the East, which was encountering concerted and determined opposition on the part of the old alliance: Great Britain, Russia, Austria and Prussia. To avoid becoming embroiled in hostilities, France was compelled to curb its ambitions in Egypt, which had once more exceeded its power to fulfil them – a setback that might easily have placed the regime in political jeopardy. A further consideration was that recovering Napoleon's remains could be guaranteed to take the wind out of the sails of the Bonapartists, in other words, those who espoused the re-establishment of Napoleonic rule under the leadership of Louis Napoleon, the Emperor's nephew. Although Louis Napoleon had miserably failed to engineer an amateurish *coup d'état* at Strasbourg only four years earlier, the government had unmistakably conveyed that it considered the Bonapartists a threat to its existence by summarily releasing the ringleader of this abortive attempt to overthrow it and declining to charge him with high treason.

Louis Philippe justified his eventual change of heart to a woman friend by telling her that, since the stream of petitions on the subject would have compelled him to make a decision in the end, he had decided to make it of his own accord.

On 1 May 1840, St Philip's Day, which was celebrated as France's national day during the July Monarchy, the King informed Thiers that he intended to make him a gift of his consent to what the premier had so strongly advocated: the return of Napoleon's remains. That being so, he was to negotiate an agreement with the British government. His son, the Prince de Joinville, a serving naval officer, would then sail to St Helena. This suggests that Thiers had wrung this decision from the King, arguing that it would finally cut the ground from under the Bonapartists' feet, stabilize the regime internally and lend it fresh lustre in terms of foreign policy.

One is almost tempted to describe this combination of very disparate motives – this Gordian knot of personal vanities, historical memories evocative of national prestige, and domestic and foreign policy considerations – as a classic 'French mélange'. At all events, no sooner had the

French ambassador requested permission to exhume Napoleon's remains and convey them to France than the British government came to a firm and unhesitating decision. It is even probable that London was highly relieved by this démarche because it facilitated the making of a gesture that promised to ease relations between the two powers, which had been badly strained by the Eastern question. Nevertheless, the British prime minister, Lord Palmerston, clearly conveyed what he thought of the matter in a personal letter to his brother. He called it 'a typically French request'.

On 12 May 1840, once the British had consented, the French government announced its plan in parliament. It took the deputies completely by surprise and was initially greeted with spontaneous enthusiasm. Later, however, restrained criticism was voiced, mainly by liberals whose uneasiness was unmistakably tinged with romanticism. One such objection: 'Far more grandeur attaches to a grave that lies beneath the vault of heaven, surrounded by a vast expanse of ocean, than to a marble tomb in the midst of a busy metropolis.' As for the Bonapartists, the only stick they could find to beat the government with was that a frigate was far too small a vessel for the purpose. In order to convey the body back to France with due dignity, a large warship should be employed, if not an entire fleet. They also criticized the plan to lay Napoleon to rest in the Dôme of the Invalides; the only place for it, they argued, was the column in the Place Vendôme or the Arc de Triomphe. The Prince de Joinville, who was to carry out the mission, remarked in his memoirs, *Vieux Souvenirs*, that he regarded his unaccustomed role as that of a '*croque-mort*' or undertaker. In the country as a whole, however, and especially among Napoleonic veterans, the announcement of the government's intention met with delighted approval.

But enthusiasm quickly wanes when the question of money rears its head, as everyone knows. The Chamber of Deputies voted one million francs to defray the expense of transportation and burial, a sum of which it could be foreseen from the start that it was nowhere near enough to cover the costs that would accrue. Consequently, a grand public appeal for donations was launched by a number of newspapers which either supported Thiers or were close to the Bonapartists in their views. Given the country's allegedly unanimous enthusiasm, the response was significant: of the Empire's former notables, Bertrand and Gourgaud not excluded, very few were prepared to contribute a sou. In contrast to them, it was the common soldiers – even wounded veterans and junior officers on half pay – who answered the appeal by scraping together a few francs. This highlighted an aspect which was bound to alarm the government: such a disparity in response could easily be misinterpreted as an indication of political sentiment and call the political system into question. After one week, when only some 30,000 francs had been raised, mostly in small donations, the campaign was cancelled by order of the government.

On the afternoon of 7 July 1840, the frigate *La Belle Poule*, commanded by the Prince de Joinville, weighed anchor at Toulon and set sail for St Helena. Her only escort was the corvette *La Favorite*. The exhumation party was led by a royal commissioner, the diplomat Philippe de Rohan-Chabot. Its members included a priest, the Abbé Félix Coquereau, a physician, a locksmith whose expert task it would be to open the various coffins in which Napoleon had been buried, and an artist charged with recording the event in every detail. Coquereau, the priest, had become known as a rhetorically brilliant preacher at Saint-Roch, the church in Paris that had played an important role at the very outset of Napoleon's military and political career. The 'guard of honour' consisted of two of his companions-in-exile: Bertrand, who was accompanied by his St Helena-born son, and the valet Marchand. His third executor, Montholon, had not been invited because he was too close to Louis Napoleon. Taking his place was Gourgaud, who had since been appointed a royal aide-de-camp and promoted to the rank of lieutenant-general. Las Cases, being loath to undertake so long a voyage because of his age and infirmity, was represented by his son Emmanuel, who had accompanied him to St Helena in the old days. Representatives of Longwood's domestic staff comprised the valet Saint-Denis, known as 'le Mamelouck Ali', the former chef Pierron, the manservant Noverraz, and the coachman Archambault. Gourgaud also insisted on taking Jacques Coursot, who had cooked for the household from 1819 onwards.

As was only to be expected, relations between the members of the party were seriously prejudiced from the start by jealousy and petty altercations about rank and status. On the *Belle Poule*, Messrs Bertrand, Gourgaud and Las Cases Jr were housed in specially constructed cabins separate from the servants' quarters. Marchand refused to accept this arrangement, claiming that Napoleon had created him a count on his deathbed – an assertion disputed by his companions. The problem was solved by transferring him to *La Favorite*, the only member of the party to sail in her. More friction arose during the voyage, however, Gourgaud being mainly responsible. He bickered incessantly with Emmanuel de Las Cases, who insisted on taking precedence over him in his capacity as a parliamentarian and member of an ancient noble family.

But the bitterest pill Gourgaud had to swallow was the quashing of his confident belief that, being an ADC to the King, he was naturally entitled to the role of *chef de mission*. He was all the more indignant when Rohan-Chabot disputed this on the strength of a sealed letter of appointment from Thiers, which he opened, as instructed, just before reaching St Helena. One infers from this that Thiers had thoroughly briefed himself on the personalities of the exiled Emperor's dramatis personae. What clinched the matter, however, were diplomatic considerations. In view of the currently strained relations between the two countries, every effort was to be made to avoid doing anything that might rub the British up the wrong way. That was why Napoleon's former companions-in-exile were expressly instructed to attend the proceedings 'as silent and uncommunicative witnesses of the exhumation and embarkation'. Volleys of curses directed at Sir Hudson Lowe or 'perfidious Albion', for instance, were to be eschewed at all costs.

This was a wise and far from overcautious measure, for even the devout and elegant Abbé Coquereau's *Souvenirs du Voyage à Sainte-Hélène*, published in 1841, heaped thoroughly un-Christian curses on Napoleon's former jailer, for whom he predicted 'immortality in disgrace'. Coquereau had clearly become a convert to the St Helena 'gospels' during the long voyage. It is easy to imagine the sort of remarks the impulsive and not overly intelligent General Gourgaud might have been tempted to make, had he been appointed to head the delegation!

The *Belle Poule* dropped anchor in the roads off St Helena on the morning of 9 October 1840, almost twenty-five years to the day after the *Northumberland* had done likewise with Napoleon on board. To his companions-in-exile, it was a profoundly moving reunion with the rocky island that had filled them with such horror and loathing and become the object of so many bitter complaints. This time, however, the scenery seemed suddenly to have undergone a magical transformation, and they saw it in a new, more friendly light. Arthur Bertrand, who had been born on St Helena, pronounced himself delighted to see its time-blackened crags, which now impressed him as majestic and beautiful. Even Gourgaud, who nursed the delusion that the entire venture was largely attributable to his own initiative, now extolled St Helena's 'good air'. Another passage in his account of the voyage stated: 'If the island has changed in respect of roads and agricultural improvements, as one can tell from the numbers of horses and cattle, and also of farmsteads, the same may be said of the climate prevailing here. In the old days the weather was generally fine and the temperatures were high. It now rained almost incessantly. Very heavy downpours descended on Longwood and Hutsgate [Hutts Gate], in particular, and it was far from warm.'

The exact course of the exhumation, which it had been agreed should take place on the night of 14 October, was laid down in detail in a document drafted by Rohan-Chabot and the British governor, Major-General George Middlemore. Once the four different overlapping coffins had been exhumed by British soldiers, the presence and identity of the corpse were to be verified by inspection in the presence of several witnesses. That done, all four coffins were to be closed again, inserted in a sarcophagus of appropriate size, which had been brought from France, and taken aboard the *Belle Poule*. Gourgaud's account states that the last coffin, made of zinc, was opened shortly before 1 a.m.

Doctor Guillard carefully removed the white satin shroud covering the dead man's body. To quote a letter written by Gourgaud on his return, those present recognized 'the Emperor in the uniform of his Guards, with his orders. He looked as if he were asleep. His hat reposed on his thighs. [...] The Emperor's handsome face was in perfect condition except for the nose, which seemed to have been somewhat misshapen by the weight of the coffin cushion resting upon it. There even seemed to hover around his mouth the sardonic smile which is also displayed by his death mask. The hands were pink in colour. Having felt the dead man's skin, the doctor pronounced the body mummified.'

It took forty-three men, toiling along a slippery track in pouring rain, to convey the huge sarcophagus, which weighed 1,200 kilograms, from the burial place on the valley floor to the road, where it was loaded onto a wagon. There it was draped in a voluminous violet pall embroidered with gold bees and fringed with ermine. The four corners of this cloth, each adorned with a crowned 'N', were held by Bertrand, Gourgaud, Las Cases and Marchand. Escorted by British soldiers and islanders, the solemn cortège made its way across Alarm Hill and down into James-town. At half past five, when it reached the landing place, the fort and the ships fired a salute. At around six o'clock, when the sarcophagus had been loaded aboard a sloop, it was conveyed to the *Belle Poule*. Three days later, on 18 October, the frigate weighed anchor and Napoleon set off on his voyage back to France.

His departure rendered St Helena one major attraction the poorer. The French abruptly realized this when they were accosted by an old British sergeant who had tended Napoleon's grave over the years. Having pre-viously made a living out of tips from those who visited it, he declared himself satisfied when promised a pension. The Pritchards, who had been renting the site of the grave and charging visitors an admission fee – they also ran a profitable refreshment stall not far away – made more of a nuisance of themselves. They and a couple named Dickson, who ran a boarding house in the Bertrands' former residence at Hutts Gate, loudly complained that they were now facing ruin. Their sole object, of course, was to extract compensation from the French government for the loss of income occasioned by Napoleon's exhumation. To avoid trouble, the Prince de Joinville met their thoroughly inopportune demands out of his own pocket.

But these difficulties paled into insignificance beside those which, quite unbeknown to them, were awaiting the members of the party on their return to France. When the *Belle Poule* reached the roads of Cherbourg on 30 November 1840, no one had been expecting them so soon and no preparations for a fitting reception had been made. Worse still, the smouldering Eastern crisis had become considerably more acute in the meantime, and the Thiers government had avoided an outbreak of hostilities only by swallowing a diplomatic humiliation that had brought national pride to the boil. Far more serious than this, however, Louis Napoleon had landed at Boulogne-sur-Mer on 6 August with a band of followers including Montholon, intent on seizing power in Paris by means of another *coup d'état*. Although this reckless venture had also been nipped in the bud, the elaborate ceremony with which Thiers had planned to celebrate the return of Napoleon's mortal remains was ruled out of court after his nephew's misbehaviour. Louis Philippe was compelled to acknowledge that it had been a mistake to wish to make this event the occasion for a great national celebration in the belief that it would finally legitimize his rule. In the light of the abortive *coup* at Boulogne, it threatened to become a Bonapartist demonstration of undesirable proportions. How could he extricate himself from this predicament with some degree of dignity?

The frying pan was exchanged for the fire. The sarcophagus was no longer to be solemnly transported to Paris overland, as originally planned, but conveyed there by way of the Seine. The great advantage of this was that it would not have to stop *en route*, thereby obviating the threat of Bonapartist demonstrations. In addition, the communities bordering the Seine were instructed that only the banks of the river were to be decorated in honour of the convoy as it passed by. To enable even these minimal preparations to be completed, the *Belle Poule* had to lie at anchor off Cherbourg for three whole days – not that this prevented a never-ending stream of enthusiastic pilgrims from hurrying out in small boats to pay their respects to Napoleon.

The voyage to Le Havre eventually began on 8 December. After a solemn Mass celebrated aboard the *Belle Poule* in pouring rain, the heavy sarcophagus was transferred via a makeshift ramp to the steamer *Normandie*, of which the Prince de Joinville took command. On board her were all the guests of honour except Emmanuel de Las Cases, who had set off for Paris on arrival at Cherbourg, pleading that his duties as a deputy took priority. Malicious observers remarked that he was only emulating the desertion of which his father had been guilty before him. The *Normandie* got to Le Havre on the morning of 9 December. The large crowd already waiting there broke into loud cheers at the sight of the Emperor's lavishly decorated sarcophagus, which had been set up in full view on the afterdeck. Despite the dank and frosty weather, its voyage up the Seine was likewise watched by countless sightseers who thronged the banks in their Sunday best in order to pay their respects to the Emperor, and the convoy was blessed by priests.

When the *Normandie* entered the mouth of the Seine she was met by a whole flotilla of smaller steamships that had hastened downstream from Paris. Among them was the *Dorade*, which was towing the specially equipped '*bateau catafalque*' on which the sarcophagus was to be conveyed upstream to the French capital. This floating platform had been decorated in a positive orgy of bad taste. Erected on its wooden deck was a bronze temple with black curtains, fringed with silver, suspended between its columns. The roof of the temple was adorned with four outsize gilded eagles holding garlands of immortelles in their huge beaks, the façade with four gilded caryatids symbolizing the Danube, Nile, Vistula and Elbe. This temple was designed to house the sarcophagus, with its richly embroidered pall. In deference to the sensibilities of the victorious powers, the forest of flags in the background was arranged in such a way that the battle honours embroidered on them were not readily decipherable. Around the temple, which could be lowered by means of an ingenious mechanism when passing under bridges, large bowls of smouldering incense were set up on stands reminiscent of classical antiquity. Ranged along the sides of the *bateau catafalque* were twenty gilded pilasters interspersed with as many plaques listing Napoleon's most important achievements. A gigantic gilded eagle situated in the bows of the vessel completed this preposterous decorative farrago.

At St.-Denis there was an easily foreseeable contretemps: thanks to the weight of the bronze temple and its considerable aerodynamic drag, the *Dorade* could tow it no further. With a heavy heart, it was decided to abandon the precious funeral craft to its fate and adapt the *Dorade* herself to carry the sarcophagus. A catafalque was hastily cobbled together on the afterdeck and concealed beneath a makeshift assortment of drapery. In addition, forty tricolours adorned with wreaths of immortelles were distributed throughout the tug. However, fate failed to smile even on this expedient. The Prince de Joinville rightly pointed out that all these adjuncts seriously hampered his ability to steer, so they were removed. It was decided simply to paint the tug's hull black and place the unadorned sarcophagus on the afterdeck. Napoleon never had any luck, either with islands or with waterborne travel.

The funeral convoy, which now comprised ten steamships, finally set off up the Seine on the morning of 10 December. The participants probably found this the most wearing part of the entire journey, for since it had been arranged that Napoleon's mortal remains should arrive in Paris on 15 December, a voyage which the steamers could have completed in a single day had to be spun out into four. Because the vessels were too small to provide their numerous passengers with sufficient protection from the persistently dank weather – the entire crew of the *Belle Poule* was also bound for Paris – they had to keep warm by imbibing generous quantities of brandy. To cut a long story short, the trip that had been planned with such solemnity threatened to degenerate into drunken hilarity. We may be forgiven for supposing that this reached its height when the convoy got to Asnières and passed the *bateau catafalque*, which had been towed there.

When the flotilla reached Courbevoie on 14 December, the long voyage was at an end. The sarcophagus was conveyed ashore and the proceedings at last took on their intended dignity. At nightfall a big encampment arose in which all the surviving luminaries of the *Grande Armée* assembled to do honour to their former commander-in-chief. Marshal Soult was a particularly moving sight. Leaning on the arm of the elder Las Cases, he spent a long time in front of the coffin with his head bowed, then straightened up with tears streaming down his cheeks. One notable absentee was Louis Philippe, who confined himself to sending two of his sons, the Ducs d'Aumale and Nemours. Also unrepresented by any delegation were the monarchy's major institutions, the parliamentary chambers and the government. This clear indication of the regime's profound and enduring embarrassment is supplemented by the fact that it had been careful to deploy some 100,000 men of the regular army in and around Paris, so as to be prepared for all eventualities.

The next morning, 15 December, the procession set off once more. This time the coffin was transported on a funeral car with a superstructure more than ten metres high. Dense crowds lined the route as it made its way from the Pont de Neuilly to the Arc de Triomphe, but no official delegation escorted the vehicle even now. Those who did so, in addition to units from the militia and the regular army, were a motley assortment of veteran ex-officers and other ranks wearing their faded old uniforms and tarnished epaulettes: grenadiers, cuirassiers, dragoons and infantrymen, Frenchmen, Belgians, Poles and Sardinians. It was a strangely moving spectacle, but macabre as well. The vast crowds of spectators lent it a dignity which might easily have been transformed into farce by the manner in which the Arc de Triomphe and the adjoining Champs-Elysées had been decorated for the occasion. The authorities had had the effrontery to adorn the former with an '*Apothéose de Napoléon*': the Emperor, attired in coronation robes and holding the sceptre and the 'Main de Justice' in each hand, stood posed in front of a throne on an enormous pedestal, flanked to left and right by two genii symbolizing war and peace. This tableau was strongly reminiscent of a fairground attraction, an impression heightened by the coloured flames that spewed from four large braziers, one in each corner.

The whole spectacle was a chaotic mixture of ill-painted scenery, plaster and papier mâché, and much genuine emotion. Few events that occurred in Paris during the 19th century have been the subject of so many accounts left by eyewitnesses, who range from literary figures such as Balzac or Victor Hugo to notables ambitious enough to bequeath their memoirs to posterity. Nearly all are at one in describing the occasion as triumphal and profoundly impressive, and quite a few of them stress that the return of Napoleon's mortal remains had offset the ignominy of Waterloo. In France, Napoleon is associated to this day with magic of this kind, which heals old wounds and restores dented pride. That is why, in French minds, St Helena is not just any old distant island but a *lieu de mémoire*, a place creative of national identity.

This was precisely what Otto Abetz, Hitler's ambassador to Vichy France, was counting on in 1940. A first-class expert on the country, he planned to render French public opinion favourable to the idea of collaborating with the occupying power by means of a spectacular *coup de théâtre*. His idea was to exhume the mortal remains of Napoleon's only legitimate son, the Duke of Reichstadt, known as 'l'Aiglon', who had died in Vienna in 1832 and was buried in the crypt of the Capuchin monastery there, and transfer them to the Dôme of the Invalides in Paris. On Hitler's instructions, the relevant arrangements were set in train from October 1940 onwards. By arrangement with Field Marshal Keitel, 'Commander-in-Chief West', the transfer and reinterment of the body, a strictly military ceremony, was scheduled for midnight on 14–15 December, or exactly a century after Napoleon's burial. The coffin arrived at the Gare de l'Est on the evening of the 14th and was conveyed to the Invalides without further ado. At 11 p.m. a *Wehrmacht* battalion paraded outside the Dôme to welcome it with full military honours. That apart, the whole ceremony took place in private. General Stülpnagel, the German commandant of Paris, had been permitted to lay a ribbonless wreath on the coffin, but that was all. The exploitation of this event for propaganda purposes by Ambassador Abetz and Pierre Laval, Marshal Pétain's deputy, did not take place until afterwards, when it received press and radio coverage.

It proved to be a total failure, however, for neither Pétain nor the French public took much notice of this 'family reunion'. The result is that, even today, many French people wishing to pay tribute to the memory of 'l'Aiglon', like the late Bernard-Henri Lévy, continue to visit the Capuchin crypt in Vienna.

6

The Empty Grave

Being shrewd operators, the Pritchards and Dicksons had promptly grasped what the new situation would mean: now that Napoleon's grave was empty, fewer visitors would be willing to pay the three-shilling admission fee, buy their lemonade or stay the night. Their only means of offsetting this drop in income was to turn the grave site itself into money by peddling it to souvenir hunters piecemeal. The bricks lining the burial chamber were removed and sold one by one. The soil in the immediate vicinity of the grave also found a market, as did twigs from the weeping willows planted around the site to lend it a more dignified appearance. The trees soon died as a result, but the soil was replenished and converted into cash. This trade in 'devotional' items must have been extremely lucrative because, then as now, Napoleonic trivia commanded a high price.

A situation of this kind could not be tolerated by Napoleon III, the great man's nephew, who headed the Second Empire from December 1851 onwards. Active cultivation of his uncle's memory, which had been transfigured mainly by the 'St Helena gospels', was an indispensable aid to the legitimation of his regime. If only for that reason, it went without saying that the 'sacred sites' that bore witness to the sufferings and death of the dynasty's founder should be wrested away from his tormentors. Moreover, French naval officers visiting St Helena had repeatedly drawn Louis Napoleon's attention to the neglected condition of his uncle's empty grave and former residence, Longwood House. The Pritchards, who owned the land on which Napoleon's empty grave was situated, had quickly scented that the change of regime in France presented a good business opportunity. Through an agent in Paris, they offered to sell the land, either to Louis Napoleon or to the French state. This transaction was initially blocked, at the end of December 1852, by a communication from the Colonial Office in London to the effect that foreigners were legally prohibited from acquiring land in British-owned territories. The special difficulty arising in the case of Longwood House was that it was Crown property and, thus, inalienable in any case.

Napoleon III having failed in his discreet attempt to finance the purchase of both properties out of his private purse, his only recourse was to submit an official request and enter into diplomatic negotiations. The French ambassador to London, Count Alexander Walewski, an illegitimate son of Napoleon I and Countess Walewska, approached his task with such skill that London very soon signalled its consent to a sale. However, matters dragged on for over a year before negotiations could begin in earnest. Pritchard, the owner of 'Napoleon's Vale', as the valley in which the empty grave was situated had long been known, gave a renewed demonstration of his business acumen: he demanded the exorbitant sum of £1,600 for the site, intimated that the price was non-negotiable, and said he was interested in a speedy sale because several other financially powerful parties had approached him, among them Phineas T Barnum, the American circus showman! It seems that, thanks to Napoleon, St Helena had lost much of its remoteness from the rest of the world.

Pritchard's extortionate demand provided Isaac Moss, the lessee of Longwood House, with a guide to the amount of compensation he should demand: a total of £3,500, of which £2,500 related to Longwood House itself, then in use as a cattle shed! Because news of the negotiations had aroused favourable echoes in the French press, the government felt it had no further room for manoeuvre and agreed to the absurd prices being asked. Early in May 1858, when the requisite appropriations of 180,000 francs had been approved by the Conseil d'Etat and the Corps Législatif, the transaction whereby 'the Emperor of the French and his heirs' came into possession of Longwood House and the site of Napoleon I's original grave could at last be concluded.

The man appointed to be first custodian of Napoleon's grave and former residence on St Helena was Nicolas Martial Gauthier de Rougemont. Rougemont had applied for the post, and his choice was an obvious one, given that he had served as a cavalry officer during the First Empire. An ardent Bonapartist into the bargain, he was being dunned by creditors, a circumstance which must have attracted him still more to the prospect of a lengthy sojourn on the island as '*Commandant des Résidences impériales de Saint-Hélène*', to quote his official title. He reached Jamestown on 30 June 1858, accompanied by his wife, an orderly and a lady's maid. The next day he betook himself to Longwood House, where, as he wrote to his superiors in the French foreign ministry, he was astonished by the 'effrontery' with which such a historic building had been employed for agricultural purposes. His indignation was all the more understandable because the authorities in Paris had assumed that he would use Longwood House as his official residence. That, he wrote, was out of the question because the quarters assigned him – rooms formerly occupied by Generals Montholon and Gourgaud – had long been uninhabitable. He proposed instead that the government should either acquire or rent Longwood New House, which was situated nearby and had caught his eye at once, thanks to its handsome, well-maintained appearance. If he established his official residence there, as he suggested, it would enable him to supervise the necessary restoration of Longwood Old House from the immediate vicinity.

But the authorities in Paris turned a deaf ear to Rougemont's insistent requests that they acquire Longwood New House and assign it to him as an official residence. Either they were unwilling to spend any more money, or they considered it inopportune to acquire a building that could not be accounted a genuine memorial site because the Emperor had expressly refused to live in it. In view of Rougemont's estimate that it would cost the exorbitant sum of £3,426 just to renovate Longwood New House, thrift would seem to be the likelier motive.

Poor Rougemont, who was compelled to put up at a hotel in Jamestown, consequently hit upon the logical idea of at least renting Longwood New House on his own account. This brought him up against the rapacious Mr Moss, who held the lease on that property. After lengthy negotiations hampered by Rougemont's lack of English, he finally succeeded in moving into Longwood New House as its sub-lessee in February 1859. He was only partially successful, however, because Moss granted him only a short sub-lease that would soon enable him to take advantage of the Frenchman's predicament by making new and increased demands.

This tug of war is indicative in itself of the incomprehension, if not lack of interest, with which the situation on St Helena was viewed by the authorities in Paris. They clearly believed that the acquisition of Longwood Old House and the grave site had sufficiently fulfilled their dynastic responsibilities, and that all that remained was to tackle the restoration of both memorial sites. Hence their rejection of Rougemont's further proposal that all the furniture and other household effects belonging to Longwood Old House, which had been auctioned off on St Helena after Napoleon's death, should be bought back and installed in their original places. Rougemont must have greatly resented the reproachful tone in which he was enjoined to stick to his instructions and confine himself to the structural restoration of Longwood Old House.

On 30 October 1858, after he had been living on the island for four months, Rougemont sent Paris a detailed report in which he estimated that there would be no shortage of local artisans available for renovation work. However, they were so unskilled that, were the government to rely on them alone, the requisite restoration of Longwood and the grave site would take at least six years. Furthermore, there was a danger that the work would be very inadequately carried out because local builders didn't even use plumb lines to ensure that walls were truly perpendicular. He therefore recommended the dispatching of an engineer officer and a company of experienced pioneers, who would be able to complete the long-discussed restoration work in short order. This information had the desired effect. On 1 March 1859, Captain of Engineers Eugène François Masselin landed on the island accompanied by his wife, another officer, and four of his men. Masselin not only had a command of English, unlike Rougemont, but succeeded where Rougemont had failed: at the end of February 1860, he persuaded Moss to grant a fifteen-year sub-lease on Longwood New House. He, his wife and his brother officer moved in there with the Rougemonts, whereas his men had to camp at Longwood Old House.

This lent another dimension to the vexed question of renting Longwood New House, for which Paris clearly had no sympathy, because so long a lease should first have been approved by the foreign ministry. Rougemont justified his arbitrary action on two grounds: first, but for this second lease, Moss would have thrown him out into the street; and, secondly, he and his family could not be expected to move into the already renovated part of Longwood House, in other words, Napoleon's former quarters, because 'the climate in this part of the island is tolerable only in Longwood New House, which, in contrast to the Old House, is situated in a dip and sheltered from the incessant south-east winds. It would thus have been impossible for Mme de Rougemont and my young family to be constantly exposed to such inclement weather in a new building.' This complaint sounds only too familiar. The result was that a substantial proportion of the funds approved for the restoration of Longwood Old House had now to be spent on renting and renovating Longwood New House. It also meant that only Napoleon's part of Longwood Old House was restored – after a fashion – whereas the former quarters of his entourage were simply demolished because there was insufficient money to finance their renovation or reconstruction.

In other words, Rougemont had arbitrarily redefined the priorities of his mission with an eye not only to his family's welfare, but also, it turned out, to his obsession with cutting a good figure socially. Instead of worrying about Longwood Old House, he devoted most of his attention to his own residence, Longwood New House, 'where Napoleon had never lived'. He converted the big drawing room into a chapel where a Catholic priest celebrated Mass every Sunday. The façade was adorned with Venetian lanterns that shed a magical light on the parties he used to throw on the big terrace, which was decorated with French and British flags on the birthdays of Napoleon or Queen Victoria. As if that were not enough, he purchased furniture and embellished the interior of his 'château' with objects supplied by the foreign ministry or acquired from Parisian antique dealers, whereas Longwood Old House, the real Napoleonic memorial, remained a gaping void. All in all, Rougemont's own residence claimed the lion's share of the public funds available to him for the upkeep of Longwood Old House.

But no one in Paris seems to have taken exception to this strange proceeding. On the contrary, the foreign ministry even sent the '*Commandant des Résidences impériales de Saint-Hélène*' some horses to mount him in a style befitting his status. It also dispatched building materials expressly requested by him for the renovation of Longwood New House. None of this changed even when it turned out, as it very soon did, that Masselin had made a thorough botch of his restoration work on Longwood Old House. In February 1861, even before Masselin had reached France after fulfilling his mission and leaving the island at the end of 1860, Rougemont was compelled to report that the walls were already displaying cracks. These, he wrote, had been caused by laudable but false economies. In his final statement of accounts, Masselin preened himself on having saved no less than 45,218.70 francs out of the 210,000 francs available to him for renovation work! In fact, this balance sheet was a pure figment of the imagination. That most of the money had been spent on Longwood New House was rendered all the easier to disguise by the fact that Masselin had dispensed from the outset with the expensive reconstruction of the '*appartements des généraux*' in which the members of Napoleon's retinue had been housed.

Admittedly, it puzzled quite a few visitors to Longwood that the rooms once occupied by Napoleon were empty save for a bust of the Emperor by Chaudet, whereas their custodian's private residence, Longwood New House, resembled a museum. But even this patent discrepancy failed to worry anyone in Paris, which leads one to conclude that no one there had any definite idea of what ought really to be done with the expensively acquired '*Domaine impériale de Saint-Hélène*'. This also explains why the authorities not only tacitly tolerated Rougemont's arbitrary approach to the administration and upkeep of those properties, but did all in their power to underwrite the extravagant social life he carried on at Longwood New House.

This is a true reflection of the problem affecting Napoleon's image in France. It was not the 'historical' Napoleon whom Napoleon III invoked during his reign, but the one the legend of St Helena had made of him: a mythical, unimpeachable figure of the same name. Thus it was his 'sacred' duty, as it were, to acquire the scenes of suffering and death to which the legend owed its verifiable substance. The notarized confirmation of the bill of sale had been a highly symbolic act, but that was sufficient; the rest was relatively unimportant. The late Emperor's relatives salved their consciences with the knowledge that they sent a gardener an annual remittance to cover the upkeep of a distant grave to which they devoted no further thought.

The only change introduced by the end of the Second Empire and the beginning of the Third Republic, which in many respects considered itself a counterpart of the Napoleonic legend, was that the pompous title '*Résidence impériale*' was dropped, and the French properties on St Helena were simply listed in the '*Tableau générale des propriétés de l'Etat*', the register of landed properties belonging to the state. All else was bureaucratic routine, which meant that the legally established obligation to maintain them was fulfilled with due economy. The upkeep of the memorial sites was thus dependent on the sense of duty and initiative of the administrators on the spot. Thanks to the paucity of the funds available to them, however, they were hard put to it even to feed their often large families.

One paragon of self-denial among the custodians of the empty grave was the '*gardien*' Lucien Morilleau. One of the pioneers who had accompanied Masselin to St Helena in 1859, he stayed on after Masselin's departure at the end of 1860 and married a local woman on whom he fathered twelve children. Jean-Claude Mareschal, who succeeded Rougemont in the spring of 1868, initially appointed Morilleau '*sous-gardien*' of Longwood

Old House, where he moved into Las Cases's former quarters, the silver room and the kitchen, with his wife and increasing brood of children. In order to make ends meet, he and Mareschal, who lived at Longwood New House like his predecessor, albeit in more modest style, rented Deadwood and Black Field, on which they grew agricultural produce for sale to the British garrison. In May 1880, Mareschal abandoned this more than frugal way of life and returned to France. Bureaucratic logic prescribed that Morilleau, who stayed behind, should be appointed administrator of the *domaine* in his place, and he and his family moved into Longwood New House. When ex-Empress Eugénie, Napoleon III's widow, visited Longwood on 12 July 1880, she presented Morilleau with the only token of appreciation he ever received for his truly self-sacrificing activities: a gold brooch and a signed photograph of her son, who had been killed in South Africa.

It was mainly owing to Morilleau's unstinting efforts – he retained the administrator's post until his death in February 1907 – that Longwood Old House, which had been so inadequately restored by Masselin, remained in a reasonable state of repair. This situation changed abruptly when his successor, Henri Roger, got to St Helena in January 1908. For one thing, Roger regarded himself primarily as a diplomat. For another, although the island's importance had rapidly declined since the opening of the Suez Canal in 1869, he nursed the delusion that, as the Third Republic's representative, he could entertain high-ranking visitors in Rougemont style. Last but not least, he had almost no connection with Napoleon's memory. Lord Curzon, the Viceroy of India, who stayed at Longwood immediately after Roger took up his post, left a graphic account of his total ignorance. In view of his inability to explain the significance of the various rooms in the imperial exile's residence, Curzon jocularly suggested taking over the job himself.

Lord Curzon's anecdote is symptomatic of the very different degrees of interest devoted in Britain and France to Napoleon in general and his period of exile on St Helena in particular. Lord Rosebery's highly successful *Napoleon: the Last Phase*, published in London in 1900, was the very first well-documented account of Napoleon's detention. The book caused a furore for two reasons: not only was its author the leader of the Liberals and an ex-premier (1894–5), but he took a very critical view of the behaviour of the British government of the time, and of Sir Hudson Lowe, the jailer it had dispatched to St Helena. In so doing, Lord Rosebery added a new and sensational footnote to the overwhelmingly favourable view of Britain's former deadly foe taken by British writers ever since the publication of Sir Walter Scott's monumental *Life of Napoleon Buonaparte* in 1827. Although Rosebery's book appeared in France as early as 1901, it was not until the beginning of the 1930s that it found a wider resonance there, as the works of Ernest d'Hauterive or Octave Aubry bear witness.

In contrast to this, Henri Roger's administrative incompetence was characteristic of the distinct lack of interest in Napoleon displayed for political reasons by the Third Republic. The obvious inference is that Roger's ignorance and inactivity were perfectly in tune with the covert intentions of those who appointed him. His reports to Paris limited themselves to bemoaning the hardships of living on St Helena suffered by himself and his wife and eight children. He deplored his wife's '*débilité physique*' and '*neurasthénie*', complained incessantly of the inactivity to which he was condemned in this '*poste record de tout repos*', and informed his superiors that he had come to the conclusion that 'the function of a curator of Longwood Old House and Napoleon's Vale now lacks all utility. One simple guardian and one labourer are quite sufficient to look after this property.'

In view of Roger's idea of his job, it is unsurprising that Longwood Old House, which his predecessor had left in good order, quickly deteriorated. We can gain some idea of its condition from the island authorities' polite refusal of Roger's offer of Longwood Old House as temporary accommodation for the shipwrecked crew of the *Papanui*, which ran aground off Jamestown in September 1911. However, over two years were to pass before it became known in Paris that, discounting its historically important rooms, Napoleon's residence-in-exile resembled a ruin; that its leaky roof and broken windows offered no resistance to wind and weather, and that the damp inner walls were beginning to crumble. Early in November 1913 St Helena received a visit from the French warship *Jeanne d'Arc*, whose officers and men made an excursion to Longwood. What they saw of the house prompted the captain to write a detailed account of its dilapidation to which the journalist Albéric Cahuet, whose book *Napoléon délivré* had just been published, lent his not wholly disinterested endorsement.

This proved decisive, because in March 1914 the Chamber of Deputies voted 20,000 francs towards the restoration of Longwood Old House. Work on the building started in March 1915 and continued for over a year despite the outbreak of war between France and Germany in August 1914. There was doubtless a close symbolic connection between that conflict and the sudden haste with which this long overdue renovation was carried out: in view of France's perilous situation during the initial phase of the Great War, it was imperative to remember the country's great heroes and tend their legacy.

The completion of the restoration work presented Henri Roger with a welcome opportunity to quit his unloved post and the island he so heartily detested. He recommended that his successor as 'curator on St Helena' be 'a wounded officer no longer fit for service in the army', a piece of advice less revealing of his patriotism than of his profound misconception of – and contempt for – what his job had really entailed. Instead of complying, Paris appointed Georges Colin, who sailed from England in March 1917, accompanied by his wife and their four-month-old daughter. The *Alivinck Castle* having been torpedoed and sunk off Brittany by a German U-boat, the Colins reached the north-west coast of Spain after nine days adrift in a lifeboat. Their little daughter had died on the way, and Mme Colin had to undergo a partial amputation of both thighs to prevent gangrene from setting in. The couple spent her two-year convalescence at El Ferrol in Galicia, Franco's birthplace, before setting off again for St Helena, where they landed early in October 1919.

Although Colin's posting to the island may strike one as bureaucratically insensitive, it was logical enough. He seemed just the expert the job required, having been an engineer officer in Tonkin, where his valuable experience of managing construction projects in the tropics promised to be of great use in his new appointment. Colin ascertained immediately on arrival that the renovation work supervised by his predecessor, which had cost a total of 31,000 francs, was totally inadequate. What undoubtedly influenced this harsh verdict was the fact that, in order to save the rent on Longwood New House, Colin and his wife set up home in all of Napoleon's former quarters except the billiard room. The official reason for this step, which rendered most of Longwood Old House inaccessible to visitors, was that the couple suffered from rheumatism and could not, therefore, move into the small house in the vicinity of Napoleon's grave that also formed part of the '*domaine*'. Colin never even considered the alternative, which was to occupy the rooms in which Morilleau and his large family had lived for some years.

It was a blatant scandal that the 'curator' should occupy most of Napoleon's former suite, the true memorial site, and simply allow the rest of the premises to deteriorate. Late in the 1920s, this state of affairs acquired a political dimension. Outraged by the abuses that had become established on St Helena, the perfume manufacturer François Coty, real name Spoturno, a native of Ajaccio like Napoleon, saw them as a favourable means of propagating his extreme views in the upper echelons of French society. Coty was an admirer of Italian fascism and aspired to implant it in France as well. To that end, he had in 1922 bought the respected daily *Le Figaro* and installed its editorial offices at the Rond-Point des Champs-Élysées, one of the best addresses in Paris. At the same time, he harnessed the newspaper's political orientation to his own extreme right-wing views. In 1928, in order to render these capable of winning a majority, he also founded *L'Ami du Peuple*, a newspaper aimed at the lower-middle classes, unlike *Le Figaro*. This sold for the cut-throat price of ten centimes, whereas other metropolitan newspapers cost twenty-five.

In 1928 Coty financed a trip to St Helena by the journalist and Napoleon enthusiast Ernest d'Hauterive and a friend of his, the architect Marcel Gogois, their task being to form an authoritative impression of the dilapidated state in which the memorial sites were reported to be. On his return, d'Hauterive launched a spirited press campaign which was fully in line with Coty's intentions. In an article for the *Revue des Deux Mondes*, which was then obligatory reading for members of the Parisian salons, he gave the following description of the conditions he encountered in Longwood Old House: 'It saddens and amazes one to note that the Emperor's quarters, those rooms in which he spent such mournful hours, rooms rendered famous by his presence – that this wretched interior is now used as the curator's abode! He occupies the bedroom, workroom, dining room and library. His furniture is everywhere. All that remain empty and accessible to visitors, who do not get to see any other rooms, are the drawing room and the anteroom immediately adjoining it. [...] This is a scandal which must be brought to an end without delay.'

A summary of this article promptly appeared in *Le Figaro*, and at the end of October Coty's campaigning daily, *L'Ami du Peuple*, published an open letter from d'Hauterive announcing the foundation of the 'Amis de Saint-Hélène', an association whose principal purpose would be the reconstruction of those parts of Longwood House which had been occupied by Napoleon's companions but demolished during the restoration work of 1860. The new buildings would become the home of the curator, who could then vacate the Emperor's quarters proper, in which he was currently residing. Longwood's original appearance would thus be restored, and visitors could once more view all the places that testified to the prisoner's protracted sufferings.

Founded two years later, the association was financially well-equipped thanks to a donation of 500,000 francs from Coty, coupled with an undertaking that more such contributions would follow. This money was used to carry out the planned additions to Longwood House, which were entrusted to Gogois. With the aid of prefabricated structural components, he was able to complete the project by the middle of 1934. Although this fulfilled the purpose of the association, the hopes pinned on it by Coty, in particular, came to nothing: the French public took absolutely no notice. It made no difference that the then British governor of St Helena, Sir Stewart Spencer Davis, offered to return all the pieces of furniture that had formerly stood in the '*Grand Empéreur*'s' suite of rooms, but had, since his death, been utilized in Plantation House or the Castle. This donation, which formed the basis of the Longwood Old House museum, was continuously augmented from the late 1950s onwards by further purchases of original household effects, contemporary articles, and replicas.

But the most noteworthy aspect of this museum initiative is that it came from the British, not the French side. The avowed purpose of the 'Amis de Sainte-Hélène', the association inspired and financed by Coty, had been merely to render the rooms in Longwood House, which were empty save for Chaudet's bust of Napoleon, accessible to the public. It did not become the association's express policy to restore them to an approximation of their original appearance and develop the house into a museum until 1935, when criticism was levelled at its architecture and, yet again, at the imperfect workmanship of the annexes. The association was past saving, however, because the additional contributions Coty had promised did not materialize. And this, in turn, was the principal reason why the 'Amis de Sainte-Hélène' soon lost their initial enthusiasm for the project, which had been inspired mainly by the lavish banquets served at their meetings.

The association's empty coffers promptly put a stop to any further development of the Napoleon museum initiated by the governor's contributions, especially as the Third Republic remained true to its traditional policy of neglect and made no move to release any funds. All the authorities deigned to do was dispatch a French naval training ship to St Helena with a cargo of 'Elen', a miracle product for use against the termites to which Longwood Old House had since fallen prey. The purchase of this poisonous substance, which had the desired effect, swallowed up the last of the association's funds.

Thereafter Longwood Old House relapsed into its Sleeping Beauty mode, the more so since the curator, Georges Colin, had finally lost all interest in his job and was preoccupied solely with his failing health. This attracted no attention because all activities on the island were brought to a standstill by the outbreak of the Second World War and the defeat and occupation of France. It did, however, prove particularly unfortunate as regards the termites, which had been successfully tackled with 'Elen', because the product had to be applied every six months in order to assure timber-framed Longwood Old House of lasting protection.

The consequences of this neglect were only hinted at in a report which the new curator, Georges Peugeot, sent the French foreign ministry in mid-October 1945: 'The house is in a lamentable condition. If it remains in its present state, the tourists of all nationalities who come to visit it will leave the island with a very poor impression, for although it is clear that the house is undergoing repairs, one cannot fail to notice that the exterior and interior are in a deplorable state.' In a letter to his predecessor, Colin, Peugeot confessed that he had felt awkward about sending the ministry a detailed report because the defects were such that they could not all have originated since Colin's own last report in December 1943 ...

Ironically enough, it was another British intervention which preserved the Napoleonic memorials from the threat of utter ruin in consequence of France's dire post-war situation. King George VI, who put in at St Helena on his way back from a trip to South Africa accompanied by his wife and two daughters, Elizabeth and Margaret, paid a visit to Longwood Old House. Although it had been lavishly decorated for the occasion, the destruction wrought mainly by termites could not be concealed. To their surprise, the royal couple found themselves confronted, not by an imperial residence, but by a ruin with a tricolour fluttering over it in the trade wind. On his return to London, the King summoned the French ambassador, described his impressions of '*la maison de l'Empéreur*', and expressed the hope that the French government would do all that was necessary to restore the building thoroughly. This admonition finally had the desired effect: at long last, ninety years after acquiring the properties on St Helena and converting them into Napoleonic memorials, any previous efforts to preserve them having been purely cosmetic and thoroughly inadequate, the French Republic consented to undertake the complete restoration and reconstruction of Longwood Old House.

As early as July 1947, the state 'administrator of domains' dispatched an architect to St Helena who estimated that the work to be carried out would cost approximately sixty million francs. In the event, Peugeot had to make do with the twenty million that were finally approved in March 1950. In February 1955 he was able to report that the work had been completed. This meant, *inter alia*, that the building's timbers had been replaced *in toto*, the roofs relaid, and all the walls stabilized or rebuilt. The wooden panelling, too, had had to be completely reproduced in its original form, and teak parquet flooring had been laid in all the rooms formerly used by Napoleon. In short, the building had been completely reconstructed, not simply restored, which says much about its previous condition. The ceremonial reopening of Longwood Old House took place on 27 March 1955, an occasion which the postal authorities of St Helena celebrated by issuing a ten-shilling stamp depicting the building. The island's postage stamps have featured the house on several subsequent occasions, whereas the French post office has hitherto refrained from doing so.

Since 1956 the curatorship of the French properties on St Helena has been held, *de père en fils*, by Gilbert and Michel Martineau, of whom the latter has been *en poste* since 1987. It is thanks mainly to their efforts that Longwood Old House is now an immaculately maintained and, despite a whole series of further extensive and expensive renovations, most authentic-looking memorial. The complex was augmented in 2003 by a museum housed in two buildings constructed in 1935, which had hitherto accommodated the curator's office and official residence.

What largely facilitated this, however, was that, shortly after Gilbert Martineau took over the curatorship, and after almost a century during which the Napoleonic legacy on St Helena had suffered from a pronounced lack of interest, a fundamental change took place in France itself. This is associated mainly with the name of General de Gaulle. As the first and well nigh all-powerful president of his personal creation, the Fifth Republic, he made frequent and emphatic references to the greatness of France. In order to demonstrate this and, more especially, to impress it on the French after their traumatic experiences in the recent and very recent past, de Gaulle's minister of culture, André Malraux, initiated a new cultural policy. Apart from its unmistakably historico-political features, it differed from the 'long' Third Republic's approach in displaying no fear of contact with France's Napoleonic legacy. And that oft-suppressed connection is more clearly apparent on far-off St Helena than anywhere else in the world.

There is an ironical but unavoidable twist to the story, however: the more exemplary the conservation of the scene of Napoleon's erstwhile martyrdom, to which the 'gospels' so verbosely and plaintively bear witness, and the greater the contrast between Longwood House, enclosed by its well-kept gardens, and the humdrum appearance of Longwood itself, which is concealed from view by the shrubs and tall trees that flank the property to the south-west, the more the 'truth' of the tragedy alleged to have unfolded there evaporates. Today, this lovingly tended scene is evocative less of martyrdom than of the refinement still characteristic of 19th-century Europe. Those who seek to indulge their nostalgia in the atmosphere of a bygone age will satisfy it here, of all places, in this remote spot on St Helena in the South Atlantic. Longwood Old House will inevitably inspire them with a more vivid sense of being in a time warp than any of Goethe's former homes in Frankfurt or Weimar.

7

From 'Devil's Island' to
Millionaires' Playground?

What to do with an island that possesses no military or commercial value, is devoid of scarce raw materials, and has nothing to offer but a bizarre alternation of rugged mountains, fertile valleys and barren plains? That question arose long ago, at latest since the opening of the Suez Canal in 1869 and the development of steamships big and fast enough to exempt them from having to make an intermediate stop at St Helena to take on fresh water. Technological advances in transportation since the time of Napoleon's exile have thrust the island back into the limbo in which it reposed during the first few years and decades after its discovery by the Portuguese.

This process was vastly accelerated by the Second World War, especially as the only place to benefit from that conflict was Ascension, which lies some 700 miles north-west of St Helena just south of the equator. Although it is a small and inhospitable volcanic island resembling a moonscape, its topography lent itself to the construction of an airfield used by the Americans as a staging post for long-range aircraft on their way to the North African theatre of operations.

Wideawake Airfield is still an American air base housing the 'Southeast Tracking Station' of the 'USAF Eastern Test Proving Ground', in other words, the control centre in the target zone of a remote area used for rocket-testing. Apart from aircraft belonging to the US Air Force, which come from Patrick Air Base in Florida, the only planes permitted to use the airfield are the RAF machines that land there twice weekly on their way from Brize Norton, Oxfordshire, to Port Stanley in the Falkland Islands. Any civilian who manages to wangle a seat on one of those flights, which greatly reduce the travelling time to St Helena, flies with an airline styling itself the Ministry of Defence!

The runway of Wideawake Airfield is so closely flanked by two volcanic cones, you feel your RAF Tristar's wings are going to scrape them. It is reputed to be the longest in the southern hemisphere. This, so the inquisitive visitor is informed, is because it could be used as an emergency landing strip for space shuttles – not that it ever has been to date. Its actual use is betrayed by the dull roar as mighty turbine engines are put into reverse thrust by the huge transport planes that land there to refuel night after night, only to disappear once more – where to, heaven alone knows – like shadowy aerial leviathans outlined against a starry sky.

In addition to Wideawake Airfield, the Americans have bequeathed the barren island a large number of big white golf balls containing sensitive aerials. The huge radio mast NASA erected on an extinct volcanic cone in 1967 in order to monitor the moon landing – for which rehearsals were held on Ascension, incidentally – is now just a prominent but redundant landmark. Of far more martial appearance, though doubtless serving far more peaceful purposes, are the tall pylons concentrated in the northern part of the island, which support a big expanse of mesh the size of several football pitches. Composed of steel wire at least the thickness of a finger, these aerials have been transmitting BBC radio programmes to Africa and Latin America since 1966. The island's third major organization, which has been established on Ascension since 1898 and 'governed' the island from 1922 to 1964, when that function was taken over by a British administrator subordinate to the governor of St Helena, is the British Cable & Wireless Company, which transferred its main base of operations from St Helena to Ascension in the 1960s. The fourth and most mysterious institution whose aerials can be seen on the island goes by the enigmatic name 'Composite Signals Organization' (CSO). This can be identified with the 'big eyes and ears' of the British foreign intelligence service, which monitor telephone, fax and Internet traffic in Africa and Latin America with due discretion and forward the data they glean to England for evaluation.

ESA, the European Space Agency, also maintains a small tracking station which monitors the orbits of Ariane rockets launched at Kourou in French Guiana until they disappear beyond the range of its radar screens. The handful of technicians who operate this station on the rocky north-east coast are Cable & Wireless employees and British citizens, but speak perfect French. If one didn't know already it, one would guess: Ascension is a restricted military area, and no unauthorized person can set foot there without special permission from the relevant British authorities.

Thanks to the great strategic importance of Ascension, which is extremely inhospitable compared to St Helena (drinking water is supplied by the BBC, which operates a desalination plant), its future seems assured. St Helena's past history, which is almost exclusively associated with the name of Napoleon, counts for nothing in comparison. Longwood House has not become the goal of the endless processions of pilgrims envisioned by Heinrich Heine. This shows, once and for all, that Napoleon was not the religious founder the 'gospels' sought to make him. He lost that very last battle as well.

But Napoleon's spectacular banishment to St Helena remained inconsequential in another respect, because it was decades before anyone remembered the island's suitability as a prison. This stemmed less from a dearth of any troublemakers of his calibre than from sober financial considerations: Napoleon's costly exile had amply demonstrated that St Helena was an ideal but extremely expensive place of internment. That was why the island was not re-employed as such until 1890. After his abortive uprising in 1888, the Zulu chief Dinizulu and two of his uncles were interned on St Helena with their families. This was the most spectacular event to have occurred there for decades, for life on the island was more than ever evocative of what Las Cases had written on 25 February 1816: 'Our days went by in complete apathy, were colourless and left only vague recollections behind.'

The Zulus were at first accommodated at Rosemary Hall in the interior of the island, an idyllic country house once coveted as his residence by Napoleon, before being moved at their own request to Maldivia House in Jamestown. Their exotic customs proved a rich source of island gossip. Far more importantly, however, their seven-year detention entitled them to an annual maintenance allowance of around £1,000 – a comparatively derisory sum, but one that provided poverty-stricken St Helena with a very welcome financial boost. Equally welcome was the fact that, from 1900 to 1902, some 6,000 Boer prisoners of war were interned in two big tented camps set up on Deadwood Plain and in Broadbottom Valley, and that 1,500 British troops had to be transferred to St Helena to guard them.

Within a very short time, their presence expanded the island's population to over 10,000 souls whose provisioning had to be ensured by a substantial increase in imports of foodstuffs and other commodities. All this helped to revive the island's depressed economic situation. The quayside at Jamestown was piled high with goods that had to be transported into the interior by hundreds of donkeys or on carts hauled by oxen. At the same time, the local farmers and fishermen profited from an enormous increase in the demand for labour, fresh fruit and vegetables, meat and fish. Meanwhile, two or more steamships always lay at anchor in the roads. In short, Jamestown pulsated with life like a gold-rush town, leading many of its inhabitants to delude themselves that 'the good old days' – the days before the opening of the Suez Canal – had suddenly returned.

However, their optimism was dampened by two occurrences. One was the exceptional drought that afflicted the island from 1900 to 1902, resulting in much-reduced harvests at a time of increased demand and a consequent rapid rise in the price of potatoes, a staple food on St Helena. The other was the typhus epidemic of 1902, which raged mainly in the POW camps but affected the indigenous population as well. This epidemic prompted the British authorities to propose transferring 2,000 or more prisoners to the Caribbean island of Antigua – a plan that naturally displeased the islanders, who were apprehensive of a check to their economic upswing. However, the plan was thwarted by the armistice that ended the Boer War, which presaged a swift end to St Helena's short-lived boom because the prisoners could now be sent home in batches. Two days after the last contingent left the island on 21 October 1902, the *St Helena Guardian* urged its readers not to forget that they had all profited from the Boers' presence. The beneficiaries included landowners, merchants and even children, who had gone to school instead of earning pocket money by working on the quayside. Indeed, the island had been positively deluged with money, and the local government had chalked up a big surplus thanks to its increased customs revenue. Most islanders, if not all, had earned more money than ever before. It was an indisputable fact that the internment of the Boer prisoners of war had brought a marked improvement in the island's finances.

All that now bears witness to St Helena's sudden but short-lived prosperity is a singular monument, visible from afar, on the flank of the range of hills bordering Deadwood Plain in the west: some huge stone steps reminiscent of an uncompleted amphitheatre. Standing at the foot of this curious arrangement are two marble columns with pyramidal tips. On going closer to the mysterious steps, one sees that each row is divided into a dozen rectangles separated from one another by a ridge of whitewashed cement and bearing a series of consecutive numbers. Seats in an open-air theatre? What militates against such an assumption is that each rectangle is covered with jagged lava chippings on which no one would care to sit. The answer to the enigma is supplied by the two columns, engraved on which are some Dutch-looking names, each with a number next to it. This strange place is the cemetery in which Boers who died in captivity were buried, most of them probably victims of the typhus epidemic that proved most virulent in Broadbottom Camp.

A curious form of piety, to identify the dead by numbers and individualize them only by means of a list carved in stone. A more cogent illustration of the grim sobriety of cultural Protestantism would be hard to find. This could be the Valley of Jehoshaphat, in which the trumpet rang out to signal the Day of Judgement. Cattle were grazing nearby on the day I visited the place. A flock of birds in a clump of trees concealing a neo-Gothic chapel flew off at my approach, protesting angrily, and clouds propelled by the trade wind transformed the plain into the stage of a shadow theatre. Profound silence reigned – or rather, the 'white noise' audible when a blank audio cassette is played. I was reminded of *Krapp's Last Tape*. An ideal place in which to stage Samuel Beckett's eschatological plays in an open-air setting. The audience had taken their seats over a century before, the 'end game' could begin. I shivered despite the scorching sun.

The Boers were followed by some more Zulus. In June 1907, twenty-five of them reached St Helena after being sentenced to long terms of detention for an attempted uprising. They were imprisoned in the fort on Ladder Hill. Their arrival brought the island no new 'gold rush', which was why the *St Helena Guardian* hastened to dispel any such illusions by publishing the regulations governing their food rations. Every prisoner was entitled to twelve ounces of 'mealy meal' (a kind of maize porridge) for breakfast and lunch; for supper, some twenty ounces of the same plus salt and vegetables; and a weekly allowance of eleven pounds of fresh beef. Tea, coffee, milk and tobacco were not provided. This account of the prisoners' meagre and monotonous diet prompted the editor to ask whether, in view of the prison regime imposed on the Zulus, the rest of the world would remember St Helena as an 'island of historical misfortune'.

It is apparent from this question that the islanders were tired of St Helena's reputation as a place of imprisonment. Despite this, the Sultan of Zanzibar, plus retinue and harem, were held captive in a building opposite the Castle on the Military Parade Ground from 1917 to 1921. He and his entourage disapproved of the island's social life and preferred to keep to themselves, so only dim memories of them have survived. The *St Helena Guardian* made no reference to these exotic 'guests'. One infers that, in their case, consideration for political sensibilities had subjected the paper to strict censorship.

The last prisoners to be deported to St Helena were a group of three conspirators from the Sultanate of Bahrain whose abortive *coup d'état* had earned them fourteen years' imprisonment in November 1956. The ruler of

Bahrain, Sheikh Salman bin Hamas Al Khalifa, had requested the former British protecting power to intern the convicted men in some territory belonging to Great Britain. The oil sheikh's request could not be rejected for diplomatic reasons, so the men were transported to St Helena on the basis of a colonial law of 1869, which expressly sanctioned the deportation of offenders from the colonies. They were confined in a building specially adapted for the purpose, the two-storeyed lighthouse at Munden's Point, a steep, rocky eminence north-west of James Bay.

Their term of imprisonment came to a premature end in 1961, after one of the internees had invoked the right of habeas corpus established by the act of 1679. A judicial review found that the application of the act of 1869 was illegal because it had no validity in Bahrain. Since this ruling applied to the other two prisoners as well, all three were promptly released and sailed for England on the next available ship. The same ruling will in future preclude St Helena from being used as a place of imprisonment for persons under sentence in third countries. Whether this applies to prisoners of war is open to doubt, as Napoleon's case demonstrates. Having gone aboard a British ship of his own free will, he was forbidden to set foot on British soil. From his point of view, that would have been the vital prerequisite for invoking the Habeas Corpus Act – successfully, in all probability.

Subsequent attempts to secure Napoleon's release by British admirers such as Capel Loft or Lord and Lady Holland came to nothing because in 1816 the government got Parliament to pass a bill tailored to fit his particular case. It legalized Napoleon's lifelong internment by assigning him the status of a prisoner of war unable to invoke a constitutional act that would have guaranteed his personal liberty. This special law, a legal expedient dictated by political opportunism, was probably unconstitutional and illegal for two reasons: for one thing, there are obvious constitutional objections to passing laws occasioned by special cases and applicable to them alone; and, for another, the detention of any prisoner of war ends when peace is formally concluded.

Far from being a mere illusion, the sense that time has stood still on

St Helena is a fact for which numerous items of evidence can be found. The most important is that, until very recently, people clung to the long-outdated idea that the island should be regarded simply as a naval base, not as a colony capable of self-development. However, the prerequisites that would entitle it to the former status have not existed for well over a century. This is reflected in the fact that the British government has to subsidize St Helena to the tune of more than £1,500 per annum per head of the population.

Potential methods of escaping from this poverty trap are not only few but unencouraging, especially as they have been tried in the past with a lamentable lack of success. That applies particularly to agriculture and fishing. Attempts to step up production soon came to nothing because the cost of transporting produce over such long distances inevitably rendered the island's exports uncompetitive. Its future is now to be based on tourism. In 2005, the British government at last consented to finance and construct the airport the islanders have long been pressing for. This project is scheduled to be completed by 2010. St Helena is to acquire a runway 2,250 metres long, but a glance at the island's rugged topography discloses that the only practicable site for it is Deadwood Plain to the north of Longwood House, from which it would be clearly visible. The runway would accommodate medium-sized aircraft capable of covering the distance between St Helena and South Africa in approximately five hours.

This international air link would deliver St Helena from its 'splendid isolation'. Whether it would fulfil the islanders' ambitious expectations of an economic boom founded on tourism, on the other hand, is another matter. Apart from its picturesque scenery, a genuine abundance of natural beauty, a very pleasant climate and its Napoleonic memorabilia, St Helena has little to offer that would tempt anyone to make such a long, expensive and tiring journey to such a remote part of the world. Although the island has boasted a golf club for over a century, there are almost no sandy bathing beaches except Prosperous Bay in the east and Sandy Bay in the south. As for the island's three hotels, all of which are in Jamestown, the demanding visitor would find them far from satisfactory.

Thus there are many indications that St Helena will remain what it always has been: one of the most out-of-the-way and inaccessible but beautiful islands in the world; not a 'wart' but a *grain de beauté* – a beauty spot, as the gallant French call it – on the vast expanse of the South Atlantic. Perhaps this is as it should be, for not even the great Napoleon's tribulations and death have succeeded in delivering this Sleeping Beauty from the curse of sheer isolation.